RUDOLF STEINER (1861–1925) called his spiritual philosophy 'anthroposophy', meaning 'wisdom of the human being'. As a highly developed seer, he based his work on direct knowledge and perception of spiritual dimensions. He initiated a modern and universal 'science of spirit', accessible to anyone willing to exercise clear and unprejudiced thinking.

From his spiritual investigations Steiner provided suggestions for the renewal of many activities, including education (both general and special), agriculture, medicine, economics, architecture, science, philosophy, religion and the arts. Today there are thousands of schools, clinics, farms and other organizations involved in practical work based on his principles. His many published works feature his research into the spiritual nature of the human being, the evolution of the world and humanity, and methods of personal development. Steiner wrote some 30 books and delivered over 6000 lectures across Europe. In 1924 he founded the General Anthroposophical Society, which today has branches throughout the world.

SPIRITUAL ECOLOGY

Reading the book of nature and reconnecting with the world

RUDOLF STEINER

Compiled and edited by Matthew Barton

RUDOLF STEINER PRESS

Rudolf Steiner Press
Hillside House, The Square
Forest Row, RH18 5ES

www.rudolfsteinerpress.com

Published by Rudolf Steiner Press 2008

Earlier English publications: see Sources section on pp. 235–8

Originally published in German in various volumes of the GA (*Rudolf Steiner Gesamtausgabe* or Collected Works) by Rudolf Steiner Verlag, Dornach. For further information see Sources, pp. 235–8. This authorized translation is published by permission of the Rudolf Steiner Nachlassverwaltung, Dornach

All material has been translated or revised by Matthew Barton

A catalogue record for this book is available from the British Library

ISBN: 978 1 85584 204 5

Cover by Andrew Morgan Design
Typeset by DP Photosetting, Neath, West Glamorgan
Printed and bound by Cromwell Press Limited, Trowbridge, Wiltshire

Contents

Editor's Note

The passages collected here are longer or shorter extracts from the larger context of whole lectures. Steiner developed his lectures into an art form in the best sense, and the reader is referred to the original, complete lectures for the 'total experience' and context from which these passages are drawn.

I would like to thank Margaret Jonas, librarian at Rudolf Steiner House, London, for her invaluable help in locating volumes used in compiling this book.

M.B.

Introduction

As I write, in November 2007, the International Panel on Climate Change (IPCC) has just issued its latest report, suggesting that the effects of climate change may be 'abrupt and irreversible' and that humanity has only a very limited period left in which to address the environmental problems it has itself unleashed.

There is no need to enter here into the tangible evidence of our harmful effects on the planet, for these have been and will continue to be described in vivid and alarming detail in almost every daily newspaper. For ages, the natural world was simply a 'given', an endless resource to be exploited with as little thought, perhaps, as we give to our body while we feel well. But suddenly, in the last few decades, we have been compelled to wake up to this unconscious, material basis of our lives on earth, and confront our own conduct. Our mother (*mater* = matter) now appears to be an ailing patient in need of our care, rather than the all-providing parent she was for so long. A century ago, during Rudolf Steiner's lifetime, the seas off Newfoundland were thronging with vast numbers of fish. You could sail out, put down your net and haul in bountiful plenty without any apparent end. Now though, as everyone knows, the cod have gone. This is just one striking image among many of the depletion and impoverishment we have brought about through a failure to live in harmony with our natural environment.

It is common knowledge that a sudden, severe illness can shock people into an awareness of how they have led their lives, and bring about radical changes in their outlook and lifestyle. This is surely what is happening now on a global level. For ever greater numbers of ecologically aware people—really it feels like a great upsurge of global awareness in the face of potential catastrophe—the time to act responsibly has arrived. Perhaps, as pessimists suggest, it is all too little too late. We are reaping the bitter harvest of our unsustainable and irreversible exploitation of the planet, the physical symptoms, you might say, of our descent into and utter belief in materialism during the industrial and now the technological age. There is of course a whole school of thought that considers the solutions to our environmental problems will be just technological 'fixes'. But while human ingenuity and intelligence will doubtless play a vital role in healing our ecological impact, it seems to me that something radically different is called for. Our whole outlook, our attitude towards the planet and ourselves is changing and has to change.

For me, this is the enormously hopeful aspect of this crisis. Of course it matters whether the patient survives—and we are all that patient—but physical survival is not, ultimately, the only or even the most important thing. As we struggle through the illness, fighting perhaps for our lives, we have to ask what these lives are, and what they are for. In other words, the crisis is also one of consciousness, a turning point when we face stark choices about our human future.

How can Rudolf Steiner possibly help us in our current situation? The word 'ecology' had not even been coined when he was speaking and writing at the beginning of the last century. The revolutions in agriculture, culture and technology that would dominate that century were still in their infancy when he died in 1925. But if we see the problems facing us as deeply connected with consciousness, his insights into humanity's relationship with the natural world are even more relevant now than they were then.

In his mediating position between two extremes, Steiner offers us a new, conscious equilibrium with nature. We are not the lords and masters of the earth, entitled to use it for our own comfortably aristocratic and exploitative purposes. But nor are we an irrelevant though devastating irritant on its surface, without whom the earth would be much better off. Instead, we are an inherent part of the evolution of the natural world from which we have arisen, which surrounds us and in which we can rediscover ourselves, just as we can find all of nature transformed within us. Evolution has brought us forth, but now, at this turning point, we must start to take responsibility for our own further evolution and with it that of the whole planet. This is really the nature of the crisis, and the daunting but galvanizing challenge that confronts us.

And no remedy, as Steiner suggests in these pages, can be found merely by tinkering at the edges or surfaces of the problem, without self-transformation. Recycling or using low-energy light bulbs is a start, but only if such actions are less the salving of conscience than part of a new, conscious reconnection. Highly practical remedies are needed, for instance in agriculture and science, and we may look to the 'professionals' or governments to provide leadership. But just as we cannot hand over complete responsibility to a doctor for curing us when we are sick, so we cannot leave this global problem to others, since it is rooted in each person's individual awareness and responsibility.

In the extracts in this volume, Steiner shows that our own, personal relationship with the natural world—rather than the knowledge of 'experts' alone—is the starting point for everything. Thoughts are realities, and have collectively shaped the world we now inhabit. Likewise, tuning more subtly and responsively to nature, becoming more alert to its fragile, wise beauty, can help us widen our narrow, self-referential boundaries. By including ever more of the world as part of us, we can start to heal the gulf between self and world which abstract thinking alone cannot bridge and, at the same time, heal the environmental harm our evolution into selfhood has inevitably caused. Here, practical remedy and inner development go hand in glove.

Inevitably, in this process, we come up against the limitations of a solely materialistic view. Time and again in these pages Steiner urges us to look higher and deeper than matter alone. Ecology is the study of living interaction within biosystems, the study therefore of subtle and complex synergies. Long before anyone had heard of the butterfly effect—the theory, developed by meteorologists in the 60s, that minute causes can lead to enormous changes in the weather system—Steiner was connecting the subtlest and most disparate phenomena. At the same time, he tried to expand our view beyond microscope or telescope to perception of non-material realities. Life, he said, arises not from substance but dynamic movement, energy and ultimately originating spirit, which attracts and condenses into material form. For him this was not, however, a vague apprehension of generalized spirituality, for he was always at pains to show the highly specific interconnections and relationships between different forms of life and to be as rigorously objective as possible in observing the minutest detail.

In recent decades, of course, dedicated ecologists of all persuasions have gone much further than Steiner was able to at the time in researching and describing human impact on the planet. But more than just prescient inklings, what

Steiner offers here is a deeply compassionate way of observing and relating to nature that can heal both it and us. In fact, as becomes apparent, it and us are one in ways we are still largely unaware of. Steiner may have died a lifetime—over 80 years—ago, but he is still waiting for us to catch up.

Part One:

PRELUDE—COMING ALIVE TO THE WORLD

1. Body, Soul, Spirit: Three Ways of Seeing

Extract from Chapter 1 of *Theosophy*: 'The Essential Nature of the Human Being'

Sensory impressions, inner emotional response and objective thinking: these three different ways of experiencing and affecting things are the foundation on which we can build our relationship to the natural world. Progressing from the first two (without denying their vitality) to a more objective understanding of natural phenomena, is the basis for our conscious and ecologically-attuned place in the world. This progress—from body to spirit, as Steiner suggests—could also be seen as an advance from humanity's infancy to responsible adulthood.

The following words by Goethe beautifully characterize one approach to understanding the human being's true nature:

> As soon as we become aware of the objects around us we start to consider them in relationship to ourselves, and rightly so, because our fate depends entirely on whether they please or displease, attract or repel, help or harm us. This very natural way of looking at and assessing things appears to be as easy as it is necessary, yet it exposes us to thousands of errors that often put us to shame and render our lives miserable.
>
> We undertake a much harder task when, in our keen desire for knowledge, we strive to observe natural objects in and for themselves and in their relationship to one another, for we soon feel the lack of the standard of

liking and disliking, attraction and repulsion, usefulness and harmfulness, that came to our aid when we were considering objects in relationship to ourselves. We are forced to renounce this standard totally and, as dispassionate and quasi-divine beings, to seek out and examine what actually is, and not what pleases us. This means that neither the beauty nor the usefulness of any plant should move true botanists, who ought rather to study its morphology and its relationships to the rest of the plant kingdom. Just as the sun shines equally on all plants and entices them forth, so too should botanists observe and survey them all impartially, taking the data and standards for their assessment not from the human domain but from the domain of the things being observed.[1]

Goethe's thoughts draw our attention to three different kinds of things and modes of experience: first the objects we constantly receive information about through our senses, the things we touch, taste, smell, hear and see; second, the impressions they make on us, which assume the character of liking or disliking, desire or disgust, due to the fact that we react sympathetically to one thing and are repelled by another, or find one thing useful and another harmful; and third, the knowledge we 'quasi-divine' beings acquire about the objects as they reveal to us the secrets of what they are and how they work.

These three domains are distinctly separate in human life, so we become aware that we are bound up with the world in three different ways. The first way is something we encounter and accept as a given fact; through the second we turn the world into something that concerns us and has significance for us; and the third way we regard as a goal to strive for unceasingly.

Why does the world appear to us in this threefold way? A simple example can make this clear. Suppose I walk through a field where wild flowers are blooming. The flowers reveal their colours to me through my eyes—that is the sensory fact. When I then take pleasure in the wonderful display of colours I turn this fact into something that concerns me personally— that is, through my feelings I relate the flowers to my own existence. A year later, when I go back to the same field, new flowers are there and they arouse new joy in me. The previous year's joy rises up as a memory; it is present in me although the object that prompted it in the first place is gone. And yet the flowers I am now seeing are of the same species as last year's and have grown in accordance with the same laws ...

Thus we human beings are constantly linking ourselves to the things of the world in a threefold way ... This shows us that there are three aspects to our human nature. For the moment this and this alone is what will be meant here by the three terms *body, soul* and *spirit* ... The *body* indicates the means by which the things in our environment, such as wild flowers in the example above, reveal themselves to us. The word *soul* designates the means by which we link these things to our own personal existence, by which we experience likes and dislikes, pleasure and displeasure, joy and sorrow. By *spirit* is meant what becomes apparent in us when, as 'quasi-divine beings' in Goethe's phrase, we examine and investigate the things of the world. In this sense each of us consists of body, soul and spirit ...

Because of the fundamental differences between these three words it should be apparent that we can only achieve a clear understanding of them and of our own part in them by applying three different modes of observation.

Extract from Chapter 3 of *Theosophy*: 'The Three Worlds'

Building further on the idea of three modes of seeing, Steiner suggests that progress towards a more objective insight into the natural world, and into the complex and subtle laws inherent in it, requires us to supplement physical perception with the self-developed power of spiritual vision. This does not remove us from nature, but integrates us more fully and selflessly with it.

We have seen that as human beings we belong to three worlds. The substances and forces that build up our bodies are taken from the world of inanimate matter. We know about this world through the perceptions of our physical senses. Anyone who trusts these senses exclusively and develops only sensory perception cannot gain access to the other two worlds, those of soul and spirit. Whether or not we can persuade ourselves of the reality of any being or thing depends on our having an organ of perception, a sense for it . . .

Without eyes sensitive to light we would know nothing of light or colour, just as we would have no knowledge of sound without ears sensitive to it . . .

Within our body, our eyes and ears develop as organs of perception, as senses for physical processes. Similarly, we can develop soul and spiritual organs of perception that will open up soul and spirit worlds to us. Anyone without these higher senses will find these worlds dark and silent... But we ourselves must work at developing our higher senses. Just as nature develops our physical body so that we can perceive our physical surroundings and orientate ourselves in them, so we must cultivate our own soul and spirit if we want to perceive the soul and spirit worlds.

There is nothing unnatural about cultivating the higher organs that nature itself has not yet developed, because in a higher sense everything that human beings accomplish also belongs to nature... What happens to a blind person after a successful operation is very much like what happens to those who awaken their higher senses... The world now appears to them full of new qualities, new processes and new facts that their physical senses never revealed before. They see clearly that there is nothing arbitrary or capricious about supplementing reality through these higher organs, and that without them the essential part of this reality remains hidden... We can really understand the material world only once we know its soul and spiritual basis. That is why it is good to talk first about the higher worlds of soul and spirit, and only then come to conclusions about the physical world from a spiritual-scientific point of view.

2. A Vessel for the World

Extract from Chapter 4 of *Theosophy*: 'The Path
to Knowledge'

*A fairy tale I heard as a child, called 'True and Untrue', describes
how 'True', who had lost his sight—also of course a metaphor for
insight—bathed his eyes with the dew from a certain tree, and
could then suddenly see the minutest things at the furthest distance.
This passage by Steiner, particularly its end, vividly reminds me of
that tale. We can only gain deep insight into the natural world by
refraining from imposing our own assumptions on it. In the tale,
'Untrue' pursued his own ends, foisting himself arrogantly on his
surroundings, and ultimately ending in the greatest misery and
destitution.*

One of the first qualities that must be cultivated by people
who wish to achieve independent perception of higher
realities ... is unreserved and unbiased devotion to what the
life of the world outside us has to reveal. If we approach any
phenomenon with a preconceived notion derived from our
life as it has been until now, we shut ourselves off from the
quiet yet pervasive influence this phenomenon can have on
us. While learning, we must be able at any moment to make
ourselves into a totally empty vessel into which the world we
do not know can flow. Moments of recognition happen only
when any prejudice or criticism coming from us is silenced.
For instance, it makes no difference whether we are wiser
than the person we are meeting—even a child with minimal
understanding has something to reveal to the greatest sage.

Approaching the child with any prejudice at all, no matter how wise, is like 'looking through a glass darkly' at what the child has to reveal.

Complete inner selflessness is part of this devotion to what the unknown world can reveal, and we will probably make some astonishing discoveries about ourselves when we test the extent of our own devotion. If we want to set out on the path to higher knowledge we must practise until we are able to obliterate ourselves and all our prejudices at any moment so that something else can flow into us...

We should allow things and events to speak to us more than we speak about them, and we should extend this principle to our thoughts as well, suppressing whatever it is in ourselves that shapes a certain thought, and allowing only external things to elicit thoughts...

By means of this exercise we make ourselves receptive to everything around us—but receptivity is not enough. We must also be able to properly assess what we perceive. As long as we still tend to overvalue ourselves at the expense of the world around us, we are putting off the moment when we will gain access to higher knowledge. People who give in to the personal pleasure or pain they experience through phenomena in the outer world are still caught up in valuing themselves too highly...

Any inclination we follow blindly deadens our ability to see things around us in the right light; it makes us force our way through our environment rather than exposing ourselves to it and experiencing its inherent value...

Seekers of knowledge must have the same goals for their actions as they have for their thinking—that is, their actions must not be disrupted by their personality but must be able to obey the laws of eternal beauty and truth, accepting the

direction these laws provide... In everyday life people allow
their actions to be determined by what is personally satisfying
or fruitful; they impose their own personality on the course of
events. They do nothing to unfold the truth implicit in the
laws of the world of spirit but are simply fulfilling their own
arbitrary demands. We are acting in harmony with the
spiritual world only when its laws are the only ones we
obey...

As long as our relationship to the world is a personal one,
things show us only what connects them to our own personality. This however is merely their transient aspect. If we
pull back from what is transient in ourselves and dwell with
our 'I'^{2} and our feeling of enduring identity, our transient
traits are transformed and begin to convey the eternal aspects
of things to us... Whenever I observe a stone, plant, animal
or person, I should be aware that something eternal is
expressed there. I should be able to wonder about what is
lasting in a stone or a mortal person, what it is that will outlast
their transient, sense-perceptible manifestation.

We must not imagine that turning our mind to the eternal
like this will estrange us from immediate reality and destroy
our ordinary capacity for observation and our feeling for
everyday affairs. On the contrary! Each little leaf and beetle
will reveal countless mysteries when we look at it not only
with our eyes but also, through our eyes, with our spirit as
well. Every glimmer or shade of colour, every intonation, will
remain vividly perceptible to our senses. Nothing will be lost
but infinite new life will be gained. People who do not know
how to observe the smallest detail with their eyes will never
achieve spiritual vision either, but only pale and bloodless
thoughts. Everything depends on the attitude we acquire...

3. Heightening Perception, Tuning to Natural Phenomena

Extracts from Chapter 2 of *Knowledge of the Higher Worlds*: 'The Stages of Initiation'

It is not enough just to say, theoretically, that we need to refine both our physical perceptions and understanding of nature. Steiner here outlines some aspects of a meditative practice that can develop our sensitivity for natural processes and phenomena. He urges us to pay careful attention to very subtle experiences which are really a first glimmer of the world speaking through and to us, rather than us foisting ourselves on the world. In this way we can begin to form a receptive vessel in which nature itself resonates.

Flourishing and withering

The first step is made by directing the attention of the soul to certain occurrences in the world around us. Such phenomena are, on the one hand, life that is budding, growing and flourishing; and, on the other, all phenomena of fading, decaying and withering. We can see all this going on wherever we look, and it naturally evokes feelings and thoughts in us. But in ordinary circumstances we pay too little attention to these thoughts and feelings. We hurry too quickly from one impression to another. The essential thing is that we should fix our attention intently and consciously upon them. Wherever we observe a quite definite blossoming and flourishing of nature we should banish everything else from the soul and for a short time give ourselves up entirely to this one impression. We will soon discover that a feeling which previously would have merely flitted through the soul now acquires strong and energetic form. We must then allow this feeling to reverberate quietly within us, while maintaining perfect inner calm. We must shut ourselves off from the rest of the outer world and pursue only what our soul can tell us of these phenomena of blossoming.

But we must not think that much progress can be made if the senses are blunted. First look at things in the world as keenly and precisely as you possibly can. Only then give yourself up to the feeling and thought arising in the soul. What is important is that attention should be focused with perfect inner equilibrium on both activities. If you achieve the necessary tranquillity and surrender yourself to what arises in the soul, then after a time you will experience thoughts and feelings of a new character, unknown before, rising up. In fact, the more often your attention is turned alternately upon something that is flourishing and blossoming and then upon something that is fading and dying the more animated these feelings will become. And just as natural forces build the eyes and ears of the physical body out of living substance, so the organs of clairvoyance will be built out of the feelings and thoughts thus evoked . . .

Anyone who has often turned his attention to the process of growing, blossoming and flourishing will feel something remotely similar to the experience of sunrise. And the process of withering and dying will evoke an experience comparable in the same way to the slow rising of the moon over the horizon. These feelings are two forces which, when properly nurtured and developed to an ever-increasing intensity, lead to the most significant results. A new world opens for anyone who systematically and deliberately surrenders himself again and again to such feelings . . .

Animate and inanimate

The pupil must also give further care to cultivating the world of *sound*. He must discriminate between the sounds produced by anything called lifeless (for example, a falling object, a bell or musical instrument) and sounds that come from a living creature (an animal or a human being). When we hear the sound of a bell we may associate a feeling of pleasure with it. But when we hear the cry of an animal we can discern in the sound, besides our own feeling, the expression of the animal's inner experience, whether of pleasure or pain. It is with this latter category of sounds that the pupil must set to work. He must concentrate his whole attention on the fact that the sound tells him of something foreign to his own soul, and he must immerse himself in this foreign element. He must inwardly unite his own feelings with the pain or pleasure which the sound communicates to him, and care nothing for whether the sound is pleasant or unpleasant *to himself.* His soul must be imbued only with what is going on in the being from whom the sound proceeds. Anyone who carries out such exercises with method and deliberation will acquire the faculty of merging as it were with the being who uttered the sound . . . And by this means a new faculty will take root in the world of feeling and thought. Through its resounding tones the whole of nature begins to whisper secrets to the pupil. What he previously experienced as incomprehensible noise will become an expressive language of nature herself. And whereas he had previously heard only sounds from the so-called lifeless world he is now aware of a new language of the soul.

Stone, plant, animal

First one studies different beings of nature in a particular way, for example a transparent, beautifully formed stone (a crystal), a plant and an animal. One should initially try to focus one's whole attention on comparing the stone with the animal. Such thoughts must pass through the soul accompanied by alert feelings, and no other thoughts or feelings must intrude and disturb this sharp attentiveness. We can see that the stone has a form, as does the animal. The stone remains motionless in its place while the animal changes its place. It is natural impulse (desire) which causes the animal to move, and such natural impulses are served by the animal's form—its organs and limbs are in keeping with them. The stone's structure, in contrast, is not fashioned according to desire but by forces devoid of desire.

If we think our way deeply into such thoughts, contemplating the stone and the animal with absolute focus of attention, two quite different kinds of feelings will arise in the soul: one kind from the stone and another from the animal. At first the attempt will probably not succeed, but little by little, by dint of genuine and patient practice, these feelings will arise. This must be practised over and over again. At first the feelings are present only as long as the contemplation lasts; later on their after-effects continue. And then they become something that remains alive in the soul... If the plant is then included in the contemplation, it will be found that the feeling emanating from it lies midway, both in character and degree, between the feeling that streams from the stone and the feeling that flows from the animal.

Seed meditation

Let the pupil place before him a small seed from a plant. The aim is to intensify the right kinds of thoughts while contemplating this insignificant object, and through these thoughts to develop certain feelings. First we need to realize what our eyes are actually seeing. We should describe to ourselves its shape, colour and all other distinctive features of the seed. Then we should reflect as follows: 'Out of this seed, if planted in the soil, there will grow a plant of complex structure.' Visualize this plant, develop it in your imagination, and then say: 'What I am now picturing in my imagination will later be drawn out of the seed by the forces of the earth and light. If I had before me an artificial object which imitated the seed to such a deceptive degree that my eyes could not distinguish it from a real seed, no forces of the earth or light could call a plant forth from it.' By grasping this thought clearly so that it becomes experience that is felt, you can unite the following thought with the right feeling: 'All that will ultimately grow out of the seed is already secretly enfolded within it as the force of the whole plant. No such force is present in the artificial imitation of the seed. And yet to my eyes both appear alike. The real seed therefore contains something invisible which is not present in the imitation.' It is to this invisible aspect that thought and feeling should now be directed.[3] Let the pupil picture the following to himself: This invisible aspect will gradually transform itself into the visible plant whose shapes and colours I will then have before me. Let him hold fast to the thought that the invisible will become visible, and that, if he could not think, then what will become visible only later could not already announce its presence to him.

It is particularly important that what is being thought here must also be intensely felt. The thought must be experienced in inner quiet, with no disturbing intrusions from other thoughts. And sufficient time must be allowed for the thought and feeling united with it to penetrate the soul. If this is done in the right way then, after a time—possibly only after many attempts—an inner force will make itself felt, and this force will create a new power of perception. The grain of seed will appear as if enveloped in a small, luminous cloud. In a sensory-spiritual way it will be felt as a kind of flame. The centre of this flame evokes a similar impression to that made by the colour lilac, and the edges give the impression of a bluish tint. Something formerly not seen is revealed here, created by the power of the thoughts and feelings that have been inwardly stirred into activity. The plant itself, which will become physically visible only later on, now manifests in a spiritually visible way.

It is understandable that many people will regard all this as illusion. They will say: 'What is the use to me of such visions and fantasies?' And many will abandon the path. But this is the all-important point: not to confuse fantasy with spiritual reality at these difficult stages of development; and then to have the courage to press forward and not to become faint-hearted. At the same time, however, we must continually cultivate a healthy common sense which distinguishes truth from illusion. During all these exercises the individual must never lose his fully conscious self-control. He must practise the same reliable thinking that he applies to the details of everyday life. It would be very bad to lapse into daydreams. Intellectual clarity, even sober reason, must be maintained throughout...

The following is a further exercise, to be linked to the one just described. Place before you a fully developed plant. Now fill your mind with the thought: The time will come when this plant will wither and die. Nothing of what I see before me will then exist. But the plant will have developed seeds, and these in turn will grow into new plants. Again I become aware that something I do not see lies hidden in what I see. I fill my mind with the thought that this plant, its shapes and colours, will at some point no longer exist. But the fact that it produces seeds teaches me that it will not vanish into nothing. At present I cannot see with my eyes what preserves it from disappearing, any more than I could previously see the plant in the seed. Thus there is something in the plant that my eyes do not see. If I allow this thought to live in me, imbued with the feeling that should accompany it, then in time a force will again develop in my soul which will grow into new vision. Again there will grow out of the plant a kind of spiritual flame-form, correspondingly larger of course than the one previously described. It may give an impression of blue in the middle and of yellowish-red at the outer edge.

It must be explicitly stated that these 'colours' are not colours as seen by the physical eyes. To apprehend 'blue' spiritually means to be aware of or to feel something similar to what is experienced when the physical eye rests on the colour blue...

The point is not that I arbitrarily create visions for myself, but that reality creates them in me...

Extract from Chapter 5 of *Knowledge of the Higher Worlds*: The Conditions of Esoteric Training

True knowledge of the world, says Steiner, is unthinkable without love for it. An exploitative relationship with nature is therefore only the external manifestation and enactment of a self-referential and therefore fundamentally unloving mode of thought and feeling.

We must realize that our own existence is a gift from the whole universe. How much is needed in order that each one of us may receive and sustain our existence! How much we owe to nature and other human beings!... Those who are unable to develop such thoughts are also unable to develop the all-embracing love that is necessary for attaining higher knowledge. Something that I do not love cannot reveal itself to me, and every revelation must fill me with thankfulness, for I am the richer for it...

Love for the human being must gradually widen into love for all beings, indeed for all existence. Those who fail to fulfil the above conditions will lack the genuine love for everything that upbuilds and creates, and the inclination to refrain from all destructiveness. The pupil must become someone who never destroys anything for the sake of destruction, not only in his actions but also in his words, feelings and thoughts...

4. The Soul of the Seasons

Extract from a lecture given in Vienna on 1 October 1923

One way to move on from a dry and abstract to a more dynamic, living perception of the world is to try to gain an intimate sense of seasonal changes—similar perhaps to sensing and sharing in the changing emotions written on the face of a close friend. If we stay wrapped up in ourselves and our own thoughts, it is very hard to reach out to another. Steiner hints here at a theme developed in the following passages—that the earth is indeed a living being.

But given this different orientation, not only the human intellect but also the human heart and soul will soon undergo a schooling that renders it more sensitive to impressions. It will no longer feel winter merely as the time for donning a heavy coat or summer as the signal for shedding various articles of clothing, but rather it will learn to feel the subtle transitions occurring in the course of the year from the cold snows of winter to sultry midsummer. We shall learn to sense the course of the year as we do the expressions of a living, soul-endowed being. Indeed, the proper study of anthroposophy[4] can bring us to the point at which we feel the manifestations of the seasons as we do the assent or dissent in the soul of a friend. Just as in the words of a friend and in the whole attitude of his soul we can perceive the warm heartbeat of a soul-endowed being whose manner of speaking to us is quite different from that of a lifeless thing, so nature, hitherto mute, will begin to speak to us as though from her soul. In the cycle of the seasons we will learn to feel evolving soul. We will learn to listen to what the year as a great living being has to tell us, instead of occupying ourselves only with smaller living beings. We will then find our place in the whole, soul-endowed cosmos.

But then, when summer passes into autumn, and winter approaches, something very special will speak to us out of nature. Someone who has gradually acquired the sensitive feeling for nature just described ... will learn to distinguish between nature consciousness, engendered during spring and summer, and self-awareness, which thrives in the autumn and winter. What is nature consciousness? When spring comes the earth unfolds its sprouting, blossoming life. And if I react to this in the right way, if I let all that spring really encompasses speak within me—although I do not have to be aware of it since it speaks in the unconscious depths as well—if I achieve this then I do not merely say that flowers are blooming and plants germinating, but I also feel a true concord with nature, and can say: My higher ego blooms in the flower, germinates in the plant. Nature consciousness is engendered only by learning to participate in all that develops in nature's burgeoning and unfolding life. To be able to germinate with the plant, to bear fruit with the plant, means to pass beyond one's own inner self and become one with nature. The concept of developing spirituality does not mean becoming abstract, but means following the spirit in its developing and unfolding being. And if, by participating in the germinating, the flowering and the bearing of fruit we develop this delicate feeling for nature during the spring and summer, we prepare ourselves to live in devotion to the universe, to the firmament, precisely at the height of summer. Then every tiny glow-worm will be a revelation to us of the cosmos.

Every breeze at midsummer will proclaim to us the cosmic principle alive within earthly things.

But then—if we have learned to feel with nature, to blossom with the flowers, to germinate with the seeds, to take part in fruiting—then, because we have learned to dwell in nature with our own being, we cannot help inwardly experiencing autumn and winter too. He who has learned to live with nature in the spring learns also to die with nature in the autumn . . .

But we must not die, nor let ourselves be overpowered. We can live united with burgeoning, blossoming nature, and in so doing we can develop our nature consciousness. But when we experience the dying in nature, this is a challenge to us to oppose this death with the creative forces of our own inner being. Then the spirit and soul, our true self-awareness, will come to life within us. And by sharing in nature's dying during the autumn and winter we will, to the highest degree, awaken our own self-awareness. In this way we evolve as human beings. We transform ourselves in the course of the seasons by experiencing this alternation of nature consciousness and self-awareness. When we participate in nature's dying, that is the time when our inner life force must awaken . . .

It is vital that anthroposophical knowledge should stream into the human heart and soul as a real force. This will lead us from today's dry, abstract, though precise concepts to a living, heartfelt engagement with life . . . Only the living spirit, which speaks to us in nature in the same way as the human soul speaks to us, can enter our hearts and minds in a vitalizing and uplifting way. When this does occur, our hearts will derive power from the enlightenment transformed within them, and these are the very powers we need in society.

During the last three or four centuries mankind has simply acquired the habit of considering all nature, and human existence as well, in intellectual, abstract concepts. And now that humanity is faced with the great problems of social chaos, people try to solve these too with the same intellectual means. But this will never lead to anything but chimeras. A fully developed human heart is essential for addressing social issues.[5] But no one can possess this without also finding his relationship to the whole cosmos, and in particular its spiritual attributes . . .

5. Seeing Things Whole

Extract from a lecture given in Koberwitz, Silesia, on
14 June 1924

*Ecology is, of course, the science of interconnecting biosystems, and
Steiner here makes a plea for a broader, all-encompassing view of
nature. Everything, in one sense or another, is connected with
everything else, and the narrow focus of the microscope cannot
ultimately help us to see things whole.*

The plants and animals on earth, even plant parasites, cannot
be understood in isolation. As I said before . . . it is nonsense
to seek within the compass needle itself for why it always
points to the north. We do not do so, but include the whole
earth . . . But just as we have to look at the whole earth when
we wish to explain how a compass needle behaves, so we
must also consult the whole universe when it comes to
understanding plants. It is not enough to look only at the
plant, animal or human kingdoms. Life comes from the
whole universe, not merely from what the earth provides.
Nature is a unity, with forces interacting from all sides.
Those whose eyes are open to these forces will understand
nature. But what does today's science do? It takes a little glass
plate and puts a carefully prepared something-or-other on it,
gets rid of everything else and peers at it through something
called a microscope. That is the very opposite of what we
ought to be doing if we want to comprehend the full
dimensions of the world. It is bad enough to be shut up in a
room, but now we shut out the whole glorious world with this

tube. Nothing remains but what we see through the lens of the microscope. This is what we've gradually come to. But when we are able to find our way back to the macrocosm then we will start to understand more about nature again—and about many other things as well.

Part Two:

THE LIVING EARTH

6. The Earth Being

In the following short passages, from several, slightly different perspectives, Steiner prefigures James Lovelock's Gaia hypothesis: the earth is not mere 'matter', but a living being. Infinitely complex and subtle processes are at work in the earth's dynamic organism. In particular Steiner stresses the fact that human beings are intricately connected with the earth, and that our geographical location affects us profoundly. We have to look beyond a self-enclosed sense of ourselves as human beings to a broader, deeper experience of connection with the whole earth and the cosmos that surrounds it. As adolescent humanity, we had to learn to stand on our own feet, but now—hopefully increasingly adult and responsible—we can become aware of what we owe to the earth, and what, in turn, we must do for her.

Extract from a lecture given in Dornach on 12 April 1924

Most people talk nonsense about the natural world today. For instance, they tear a plant from the ground and botanize, knowing nothing about its living context. It would be nonsense to tear out a hair and describe it on its own, for a hair can only grow on an animal or human being . . . plants are the hairs of the earth, for the earth is a living organism. And just as human beings need air to live, so the earth needs the spiritual light of the stars. It inhales this in order to live. And just as a person walks around on the earth, so the earth moves around in the cosmos. It dwells in the whole of the universe. The earth is a living entity.

The least we can do . . . is to realize that the earth itself is a

living entity. It grows young when it lets plants sprout just as
a child is young when the baby hair grows. An old man loses
his hair just as the earth loses its plants in autumn. That is a
life which merely has a different rhythm: youth in spring, old
age in autumn, youth again and old age again. It merely takes
longer in human beings. And everything in the cosmos really
lives like this . . .

Extract from a lecture given in St Gallen on
16 November 1917

One must know that our earth is not the dead object
described today in mineralogy or geology, but a living being.
Mineralogy or geology know as much about the earth as we
would know of a person if we saw only his skeleton. Imagine
never being able to see people with your senses but only by
means of X-rays; think of being familiar only with someone's
skeleton . . . Imagine coming into this room and seeing
nothing but the bones of all the members of this audience—
you would then know as much about those present here as
modern science knows about the earth.

The earth known only as a skeleton is in fact a living
organism; and as a living organism it influences the beings
who move about on it, that is, human beings. Just as a person
is inwardly differentiated in the way his organs are distributed
in his body, so the earth is differentiated in what it develops
within it, which in turn influences the human beings moving
about upon it . . . To think requires use of your head rather
than your right forefinger or the big toe of your left foot . . .

different things are distributed throughout a living organism...

And the earth is differentiated in the same way. Our earth is certainly not a being that directs the same influences and emanations to its inhabitants all over the globe. All kinds of different energy currents emerge from the earth in different regions. There are various forces—magnetic, electrical and so on, but also diverse living energies—which rise up out of the earth and affect human beings in many ways at different places on its surface, depending on geological strata and geographical conditions...

Extract from a lecture given in Berlin on 30 March 1918

From much that you have absorbed of spiritual science it will have become clear to you that our entire earth which we inhabit as whole humanity is a kind of great living being, and that we ourselves are included as part of its greater organism. In various lectures I have spoken about particular living phenomena of this being, our earth. The life of the earth expresses itself in the most diverse ways, one among them being the following. Certain relationships exist between particular regions of the earth and the human being as dweller on the earth. Just as it is true, though very superficially, that humanity is a single whole, it is also true that the parts of humanity spread out over the regions of the earth are differentiated—not only through the many influences investigated by external science and geography, but through much more mysterious influences coming from particular regions of the earth's surface. There do exist certain inner relationships, not lying entirely on the surface of things, between the human being and the soil he inhabits, the part of the earth from which he springs. This can be best seen from the fact that such relationships develop not in shorter, but over longer historic periods: for example, in the alteration undergone by European people who migrate to America and settle there. Of course, the time since America was settled by Europeans is still so short a period that only the first traces of this appears at present—but the traces are strong and definite. Life in America changes the outer form of European people, not at once, but in the course of generations. In the formation of arms and hands, for instance, and in the face, Europeans gradually come to resemble the old American Indians. You should not picture this crudely, however, but as subtler hints.

Such things call our attention in a general way to the connections between the mighty organism of the earth and its separate members, its particular inhabitants . . .

In the human being continual material processes go on that are really spiritual processes. We eat. We take up into our own organism substances from the external world. Solid materials, which are transformed into liquids, are taken into the human organism and thereby altered. Our organism consists indeed of all possible substances, which we take in from outside. But we do not only incorporate them; as we do so they also go through a certain process. Our own warmth is conditioned by the warmth we receive and by the processes through which the substances we consume pass. We breathe, and thus take in oxygen—but not only this, for since the process of breathing involves us in what happens in the external world, in the atmosphere, we participate too in the rhythm of the outer world . . . Thus through the rhythmic processes which go on in our own organism we stand in a definite relationship to our environment...

Extract from a lecture given in Dornach on 9 May 1920

As physical beings we are not a separate entity but a part of the whole earth, just as a hand severed from the human organism cannot be regarded as having a separate existence in any true sense. It dies; it can only be imagined in connection with the organism. A rose dies when plucked, and as a reality it is only conceivable in connection with the rose bush which is rooted in the earth. So, too, to understand the human being in his entirety we cannot regard him as simply enclosed within the boundaries of his skin...

7. The Breathing, Sleeping and Waking Earth

In the following two passages, continuing the theme of the earth as living organism, Steiner finds in it processes which we also find in ourselves on a smaller scale: breathing, sleeping and waking. Really to experience these processes, and their relationship to our own organism, requires an imaginative engagement with the earth which Steiner elsewhere urges us to develop. As we have seen, such imagination is not fantasy but a step simultaneously inwards and outwards: of developing our own inner perception and insight, and of relating to the greater being of which we are a part.

Extract from a lecture given in Dornach on 31 March 1923

Today let us consider this seasonal cycle of the earth as a kind of mighty breathing process which the earth carries out in relation to the surrounding cosmos ... Of course it is not air that is breathed in and out but rather those forces which are at work, for example, in vegetation: those forces which push the plants out of the earth in spring, and withdraw again into the earth in autumn, allowing the green plants to fade and finally paralysing plant growth ...

Let us first look at the earth at the time of the winter solstice, in the last third of December. At this time of year we can compare the earth's breathing with that of a person who has inhaled a breath of air and holds it in his lungs. In the same way, the earth holds within itself those forces I spoke of as being inhaled and exhaled. At the end of December it holds these forces within itself. And what is happening then with the earth I can outline for you schematically in the following way . . . We can of course only consider one part of the earth in connection with this breathing. We shall consider that part where we ourselves dwell; conditions are of course reversed in the southern hemisphere. We must picture the earth's respiration in such a way that one region exhales while the opposite region inhales . . .

Picture the time of December. At the end of December the earth has breathed in fully and holds within itself the forces I referred to. It has entirely sucked in its soul element, for that is what these forces are. It has drawn this completely into itself in the same way that someone holds breath in himself when he inhales . . .

Extract from a lecture given in Dornach on 2 May 1920

Now let us examine what is left lying in bed [when we fall asleep]. What happens to it? It suddenly becomes plantlike. Its life is comparable to what takes place on earth from the moment when plants sprout in spring until the autumn when they die back. This plant nature springs up and puts forth leaves in the human being, as it were, from falling asleep to awaking. We are then like the earth in summer; and when the ego and astral body[6] return and the human being awakes, we become like the earth in winter. So we can say that the time between waking and falling asleep is our winter, and that between falling asleep and waking is our summer . . . For the year of the cosmos—in so far as the earth is part of it—corresponds with our day. The earth wakes in winter and sleeps in summer. The summer is the earth's sleeping time, the winter its waking time. Outer perception obviously gives a false analogy, presenting summer as the earth's waking time and winter as its sleep. The reverse is the case, for during sleep we resemble blossoming, sprouting plant life, like the earth in summer...

If we now consider the cosmos, which as we see manifests waking and sleeping, we will find that we have to regard it as a great organism. We must think of what takes place in its constituent parts as organically integrated into the whole cosmos, just as what takes place in one of our own organs is integrated into our organism.

8. Macrocosm and Microcosm

Extract from a lecture given in Dornach on 16 April 1920

Steiner here links the tiny tremor of the human pulse to vast movements of the cosmos, once again giving a sense of the dynamic life informing the whole universe and human beings as a part of it.

Let us now consider a correspondence ... between the human being and the world in which he evolves. I have pointed to the fact that our rhythm of breathing—roughly 18 breaths a minute—manifests something that is in remarkable accord with other processes of the universe. We take 18 breaths per minute, which over a whole day comes to 25,920 respirations. And we arrive at the same number when we calculate how many days are contained in a normal lifespan of 72 years.[7] That also gives about 25,920 days ...

And again, when we consider how the sun moves (whether apparently or actually does not matter in this context), advancing a little each year in what we call the precession of the equinoxes, when we consider the number of years it takes the sun to make the journey round the whole zodiac once again we get 25,920 years—the so-called Platonic year.

The fact is that within the boundaries set by birth and death this human life of ours is indeed fashioned, down to its most infinitesimal processes (as we see in breathing), in accordance with the laws of the universe. But this correspondence between the macrocosm and the human microcosm is fairly evident, There are however other very important correspondences. Consider the following for example . . . Take the 18 respirations per minute, which make 1080 an hour and in 24 hours 25,920 respirations; that is, we must multiply 18 × 60 × 24 in order to arrive at 25,920.

Taking this same number as the cycle of the precession of the equinoxes and dividing it by 60 and again by 24, we would naturally get 18 years. And what do these 18 years really mean? Just think—these 25,920 respirations correspond to a human day of 24 hours. In other words, this 24-hour day is that of the microcosm, with 18 respirations serving as the unit of rhythm.

And now take the complete circle described by the precession of the equinoxes and call it not a Platonic year but a great day of the heavens, a macrocosmic day. How long would one respiration on this scale have to take to correspond with human respiration? It would have to last 18 years—a respiration made by the great being of the macrocosm.

Now taking the statements of modern astronomy—we need not interpret them here, we shall speak of their meaning later—let us now examine what modern astronomers call the 'nutation of the earth's axis'.

You will know that the earth's axis lies obliquely upon the ecliptic, and that astronomers speak of an oscillation of the earth's axis around this point, which is called 'nutation'. The axis completes one revolution around this point in just about 18 years (it is actually 18 years 7 months . . .). But with these 18 years something else is intimately connected. For we should not merely consider this 'nutation' or trembling, this rotation of the earth's axis in a double cone around the earth's centre, and the period of 18 years for its completion, but also examine another process that takes place simultaneously. The moon appears each year in a different position because, like the sun, it ascends and descends from the ecliptic, proceeding in a kind of oscillating motion again and again towards the equator ecliptic. And every 18 years it appears once more in the same position it occupied 18 years before. You see, there is a connection between this nutation and the path of the moon. Nutation is in truth nothing other than the moon's path. It is the projection of the motion of the moon so that we can actually observe the 'breathing' of the macrocosm. We only need to observe the path of the moon over 18 years, or in other words the nutation of the earth's axis. The earth dances, and in such a manner as to describe a cone, a double cone, in 18 years; and this dance is the reflection of the macrocosmic breathing. This takes place as many times in the macrocosmic year as the 18 human respirations occur during the microcosmic day of 24 hours.

So in this nutation movement we really have one macrocosmic respiration per minute. In other words, we observe this breathing of the macrocosm through nutation or the movement of the moon, and we then have before us what corresponds to human respiration...

9. Four Kingdoms of Nature

Extract from a lecture given in Stuttgart on 6 August 1908

In coming to speak more specifically of the four kingdoms of nature—the human being, animals, plants and minerals—Steiner as always hints at two things: firstly that everything—even rock—has a living dimension; and secondly, as unspoken consequence of this, that all these realms are in some way connected with us and deserve our respect and care. This view is not in the least sentimental, however. He does not personify nature to bring it close to us, but is at pains to make clear distinctions, to emphasize both difference and similarity in a rigorous way. Steiner is incapable of speaking in solely material terms of these kingdoms because for him matter cannot be understood without insight into the spiritual realities underlying it. It may seem far-fetched to speak, as Steiner does here, of minerals feeling 'pain'—but if we see everything, even rocks, as integral to the living being of the earth, and understand that everything material has a sustaining, spiritual counterpart, then perhaps we can start to conceive of minerals as being also in some way connected with all living and therefore sentient processes.

We will now go more deeply into the various conditions on our earth. We are surrounded in the first place by the four kingdoms of nature: the mineral, vegetable, animal and human kingdoms. The human being is not the merely material and physical being of which the outer senses inform us, and which the scientific intellect describes and explains, but he is a complicated being made up of physical body, etheric body, astral body and ego.[8] ... When we allow our gaze to sweep over the beings of the other kingdoms of the earth we must be fully aware that the expressions physical body, etheric body, astral body and ego are also significant in relation to them as well. When dealing with the physical world we have to acknowledge that of all earthly beings we alone possess a self-aware ego. With animals it is quite different; the ego of animals does not dwell within the physical world in the same way our ego does.

If we consider the difference between animals and human beings, we see that whereas every human being has an individual 'I' enclosed as a single individuality within its skin each animal does not have an 'I' in the same way but that a whole species shares one 'I' or ego. For example, all lions or all bears have a common ego, hence we call such an ego belonging to the animal kingdom a group ego. The human ego is found in the physical world; although we may not see it with our eyes it is present within the skin of every human being. This is not the case with animals. We do not find their group ego in the physical world. To form an idea of such a group ego, imagine that there is a partition before me, and in this partition ten holes. I put my ten fingers through the holes and move them. You see my fingers but not myself, and without much deep thought you say that these ten fingers do not move of themselves, but something hidden must be causing the movement; in other words you think of a being that belongs to the fingers. This comparison brings us to the group-nature or soul-nature in the case of animals ...

The ego-nature which in the case of human beings is present in the physical world is found in the case of animals in the astral world. The group ego of animals dwells in the astral world. From each single animal there stretches a sort of continuation of its being into the astral world, meeting and together forming the garment or uniting entity for the animal ego. These group egos live as single individuals on the astral plane, just as human individual egos do here on the physical plane. When the clairvoyant enters the astral plane he encounters the various animal egos as separate beings which extend their principles into the physical world. We should not merely picture this schematically, but accustom ourselves to picturing the reality of these egos. It must be clearly understood that we do not have to go into another region to enter the astral world; the astral world permeates our physical world. It is only a case of our being able to see into it with opened astral senses.

You may ask what group egos of animals look like. The group ego of one of the higher orders of animals appears to the clairvoyant somewhat as follows. Along the spine of the animal he sees what resembles a brightly shining line of energy. As a matter of fact our atmosphere is permeated not only by the material currents generally recognized but also in every direction by astral currents, and in these currents the clairvoyant recognizes the group egos of animals.

A second question might now be asked: Have lower beings, such as plants for example, an ego? Yes. When the clairvoyant examines a plant he finds that the part visible in the physical world is nothing but a combination of the physical and etheric bodies of the plant. Imagine the surface of the earth on which plants grow, picture the root of a plant, the stem, the leaves and flowers. What is growing there does not, like the human being, have a physical, etheric and astral body, and ego, but only a physical and etheric body. We must not conclude from this that the astrality with which we are filled, and which is active also in animals, is not active in the plant. To the opened eyes of the clairvoyant the plant is surrounded by a glow, and this comes from astral substances. It is this also which cooperates in the development of the flower. While the plant grows from leaf to leaf through the influence of the etheric body, its growth terminates above in a flower through being surrounded by astral substance.

The clairvoyant sees every growing plant thus surrounded by astral substance, but there is something else connected with the plant, namely, its ego. If we wish to locate the ego of a plant we must seek it in the centre of the earth. There the ego of all plants is to be found; this is an important and essential truth. Whereas we see the egos of animals in the circumference of the earth, we must turn to the centre of the earth for the egos of plants. In fact, when clairvoyant vision has penetrated to such a view of the plant kingdom, the earth, which otherwise confronts us merely as a material structure, expands to an organism with its ego in the centre that includes all plant egos.

The earth is ensouled by an ego; and in the same way as your head is covered with hairs which grow out of you, so plants grow out of the being of the earth, and belong to the whole organism of the earth. When one tears a plant up by the roots it hurts the whole earth; the soul of the plant experiences pain. This is a fact. On the other hand one should not think that the earth feels pain when a flower is plucked; exactly the reverse is the case. For example, when in autumn a reaper cuts corn the clairvoyant sees great currents of well-being pass over the earth. Objections to this from the moral standpoint do not hold good. One might for example ask: Is it worse when a child plucks all sorts of plants uselessly than when someone transplants one carefully and with good intention? The fact remains the same: if a plant is uprooted the earth feels pain; if a plant is cut the earth feels pleasure. The earth has pleasure in yielding up what it bears on its surface; also when animals pass over the earth, grazing upon its plants, the earth has a sensation of pleasure, much the same as a cow has when her calf draws milk . . . These are not merely comparisons, but are actual facts. Anyone who with clairvoyant vision can see into the astral world still sees nothing of the ego of plants; to do this a higher clairvoyance is required, by which it is possible to see into the devachanic[9] world.

We can say, therefore, that the group ego of animals is in the astral world, whereas the ego of plants exists in the devachanic world.

The next question that naturally presents itself relates to the mineral world. What is the condition of so-called lifeless minerals? Have they anything resembling an ego, or some other higher principle? If we observe a stone clairvoyantly we find that in the physical world it has only a physical body; the etheric body of minerals surrounds and envelops them on all sides. Take, for example, a rock crystal; you must imagine this entire form as hollowed out, resembling a hollow space, and only where the physical substance ends does the etheric begin. Just as the upper part of a plant is woven round by the astral, so the mineral is surrounded by the etheric. This etheric is at home in the astral world. Please note this carefully—we have here an etheric sphere that is at home in the astral world.

Things are really more complicated than is generally supposed. It is not the case that in the astral world everything is astral; this is as little the case as that in the physical world everything is physical. For example, interpenetrating the physical world you have the etheric body, the astral body, and

even the human ego; and the clairvoyant also sees the etheric
body of minerals in the astral world ...

So here we have a panoramic view of the different kingdoms. The ego of man is on the physical plane, that of
animals on the astral plane, that of plants in the lower regions
of the devachanic world, and the ego of minerals exists in the
higher regions of the same world ...

When a mineral is broken up it does not feel pain. On the
contrary, it feels pleasure, a sensation of well-being. Great
currents of pleasurable feeling stream forth from a quarry
where stones are broken to pieces; on the other hand, were
you to recombine and condense all the broken pieces
together again it would cause great pain. The same fact may
be observed in another process. Imagine that you have a glass
of warm water into which you throw a piece of salt. When the
salt dissolves not only does the substance dissolve but feelings of well-being fill the warm water, feelings of pleasure on
the part of the mineral at being dissolved. But if you cool the
water so that the salt crystallizes out, the process is connected
with a feeling of pain ...

Thus we can now consider the world with entirely different
feelings; for we regard the earth not only as a body shone
upon by the external rays of the sun but as a living being
absorbing the soul of the sun through the astral mantle of
plants. And we see the entire universe permeated by the egos
of minerals. We see how all these things are ensouled and
filled with spirit ...

10. Materialism Fails to Know Matter

Extract from a lecture given in Dornach on 2 February 1924

Science is traditionally most concerned to quantify physical substances and forces—to investigate matter. But this is only one aspect of the cosmos, and in fact, says Steiner, matter cannot be properly understood only on its own terms. To cite an analogy he used earlier in this volume, this is like trying to understand the compass needle's movement by studying the needle itself, not the context of forces it is responding to.

As well as gravity, for instance, there is an opposite, expanding force which Steiner here calls 'upthrust' and elsewhere 'levity', which is harder to quantify because of its more fluctuating, ethereal nature. At the end of this passage Steiner prefigures a remarkable experience which many had when spacecraft first gave us photographs of the whole earth suspended like a shining water drop in space: not just a place of dead forces, but a living, vibrant entity.

While we are held to the earth by gravity, we tend away from the earth because of the etheric.[10] It is really the etheric that is active in this centrifugal tendency. In this connection you need only think of the following. The human brain weighs approximately 1500 grams. Now a mass with this weight, pressing on the delicate blood vessels at the base of the brain, would quite compress them. If our brain actually exerted its 1500 grams weight inside the living head we could not have these blood vessels. During life, however, the brain weighs 20 grams at most. It is so much lighter because it floats in the cerebral fluid and loses in weight by the weight of fluid displaced. The brain really strives away from us and in this tendency the etheric is active. Thus we may say that it is precisely in the brain that we can see most clearly how matters stand.

Here is the brain floating in its fluid, whereby its weight is reduced from 1500 to about 20 grams. This means that its activity shares to a remarkably small degree in our physical, bodily life. Here the etheric finds tremendous scope for acting upwards. The weight acts downwards but is reduced. In the cerebral fluid there is principally developed the sum of etheric forces that lifts us away from the earth. Indeed, if we had to carry our physical body with all its forces of weight, we would have a sack to drag about. Every blood corpuscle, however, swims and is reduced in weight.

This loss of weight in a fluid is an old piece of knowledge... In physics this is called 'upthrust', and here the etheric acts. The astral,[11] on the other hand, is stimulated—to begin with—by breathing, whereby the airy element enters the human organism and eventually reaches the head in an extremely attenuated state; in this distribution and organization of the air the astral is active.

Thus we can really see in solid earthy substance all that is physical; in fluid, especially in the way it works in us, the etheric; and in the airy or gaseous, the astral.

It is the tragedy of materialism that it knows nothing of matter—how matter actually works in the several domains of life. The remarkable thing about materialism is its ignorance of matter. It knows nothing at all about the way matter works, for one does not learn this until one is able to attend to the spiritual that is active in matter and is represented by such forces.

Now, when one progresses through meditation to the

'imaginative' knowledge of which I have already spoken, one finds the etheric at work in all the aqueous processes of the earth. In the face of real knowledge it is childish to believe that all that is at work here—in the sea, in the rivers, rising mists, falling drops and cloud formations—contains only what the physicist and chemist know about water. For in all that is out there in the great drop of the 'water-earth', in what constantly rises in the form of vapour, forms clouds and descends as mist, in all the other aqueous processes—water plays, indeed, an enormous part in shaping the face of the globe—in all this, etheric currents are working. Here is weaving the ether revealed to imaginative perception when we strengthen our thinking in the way I have described.

Part Three:

A WOMB OF WATERS

11. From Flow to Form

Extract from a lecture given in Dornach on 17 April 1920

A materialistic view sees the heart, for instance, as a central pump or organ to which blood vessels and circulation are somehow secondary. In fact, says Steiner, the opposite is true: organs form in the embryo from dynamic circulatory movements. In terms of ecology such an insight relates to the primacy of water, currents and streams out of which all life arises (including of course in the embryo) and from which it continually feeds. This picture gives an enlivened sense of matter consolidating from life and movement, rather than the other way round.

Our studies of the last few days will have made it clear to you that it is altogether impossible to look upon the configuration of the spatial universe and its movements in the way adopted by modern science. For not only does it regard the universe as entirely separate from the human being, but even the separate celestial bodies, which appear to our gaze as disconnected from each other, are each treated as isolated entities; and then, in their isolation, their effects upon each other are observed. This is like studying the human organism by first examining an arm and then a leg in order afterwards to understand the complete organism from the way in which the single members work together. But you can't actually comprehend the human organism by studying its separate parts—all investigation of the human body must have its starting point in the *whole*, from which we can then proceed to the separate parts...

We must ... examine the universe in its relation to the human being. We have been sundered from this play of forces which once surrounded us and in which we were embedded. We have been extracted from this [immersion in the whole cosmos] because our present organization has placed us firmly into sensory reality. But the fact that we are really organized in accordance with cosmic laws can still be proved today by quite external experiments, if attention is paid to certain phenomena. For instance, it is by no means mere nonsense to say that certain sicknesses can be cured more quickly if the patient's bed is placed in an east-west alignment. It is not superstition but a fact capable of definite proof...

We can discover that we become receptive to celestial forces in so far as we cease to act through the physical organs—that is to say when we are, through this non-activity, more or less in a state of sleep. Children are always more or less asleep, which is why the child is much more receptive to celestial influences than an adult. As we grow up we work our way further and deeper into earthly conditions. During childhood all that is within the skin is still plastic[12] and in a state of formation. These formative powers become less and less active with the years until, at a considerably later point in life, they become very much diminished ... but the part of our being which, as far as consciousness is concerned, remains in a continuous state of sleep—such as our heart activity, our digestive processes, etc., in fact all the inner physical processes—remains under the influences of the super-physical during the whole of our life...

Expressionistic painters may portray the human being with his toe taking the place of his nose, or with one eye placed here and the other in his hand ... but they only show how little inner relationship they have with the world. These days materialistic thought has reached the point of depicting things separately when they really belong together with the whole . . .

Consider for example an important organ, the heart . . . We can see that in a certain sense it has been woven together. By studying embryology we discover how the heart is gradually woven together or configured, as it were, by blood circulation, and is not a primary form. And the same is true of the other organs. They are the *results* of these circulations, rather than their causes. Within the organs, circulation comes to a standstill as it were, undergoes a kind of metamorphosis and then proceeds further in a different way. To illustrate this, let us imagine a stream of water falling over a rock. It throws up a variety of water formations and then flows on. These formations are caused by the forces of equilibrium and motion at this place. Now imagine that all this suddenly petrifies: a skin would be formed like a wall, then the rest would flow on again, leaving behind the form of an organic structure. We would have the current passing through the structure, coming out again and flowing on further in an altered form. You can imagine something like this in the case of the flow of blood as it circulates through the heart. I can only touch on such things here . . .

12. Currents and Migrations

Extract from a lecture given in Dornach on 9 February 1924

Continuing the theme of currents and movements of water, Steiner highlights a continually recurring dynamic between opposite poles in nature—whether of salt and fresh water, or warm and cold temperatures. The tension between such opposites manifests in the myriad migrations of birds and animals. Thus Steiner illustrates how movement and life arise firstly from a whole, living context and interaction. But he goes still further to find, within the human being as microcosm in the macrocosm, a related pull between opposites. In this sense, we can say that we ourselves are also continually 'migrating' rhythmically between our inward-looking stomach and metabolic system and our outward-looking head with its delicate sense organs and, at the same time, likewise between the earth and the heavens. The connections that Steiner draws between different natural phenomena and between nature and the human being are sometimes breathtaking; but they also continually show that we can find the whole of the natural world reflected in ourselves, and so feel infinitely connected and indebted to it.

You know that the surface of the earth is only partly solid land; it is mainly a sphere of water that moves within the universe, a watery sphere, an ocean. And in general we can say that rivers have their origin or source somewhere on earth, and run to the sea. Let us take the Danube for example, which as you know has its source in the Black Forest. Or take the Rhine, which originates in the southern

Alps and flows into the North Sea. The Danube flows through various valleys until it reaches the Black Sea. Now we generally only consider the course a river takes and how it runs into the sea. We delight in rivers, but we rarely consider the tremendous significance which rivers and the sea really have for all life on earth.

We are usually able to say more about the liquid part of a human being. As I have told you, the human being is largely also a mass of fluid, one type of which is the blood flowing in his veins. We also know that the bloodstream has the greatest imaginable importance for life. Blood creates and sustains life. As physical human beings we are completely dependent on the blood flowing through the body in the right way, following particular pathways. If it were to depart from its pathways we could not live. People do not usually realize that the way the earth's waters are arranged in rivers and oceans has an equally great significance for the earth. Why don't people realize this?

We can't fail to notice the importance of blood; it is red and contains all kinds of substances, and so we tell ourselves that blood is something special. Water we think of merely as water. It attracts less attention; and the substances it contains—apart from hydrogen and oxygen—are not present in such large quantities as iron is, for instance, in the blood. So people pay less heed to it, but it is true nevertheless that the whole circulation of water has tremendous significance for the life of the earth. Just as the human organism could not live if it did not have its blood circulation, so the earth would be unable to live without its water circulation.

The special characteristic of this water circulation is that it originates in something quite different from the state it has reached when it runs into the sea. You see, if you examine rivers you find they do not contain salt; the water is fresh. Rivers are fresh water while the sea is salt. And everything which the sea causes is due to its salt content. This is extraordinarily important: the water begins to circulate as fresh, salt-free water on earth, and it ends in a salty state in the sea.

People usually consider that a river like the Rhine has its source somewhere, flows on like this and then runs into the sea. This is what you see externally. But what people fail to recognize is that the river, the Rhine for example, outwardly flowing like that from the southern Alps to the North Sea, also has a kind of energy current running below ground from the mouth of the river back to its origin. The current returns, below ground, along its course, from the mouth of the river to its source. Above ground the river contains fresh water without salt. Underground, salt is deposited along the reverse current, so that the earth receives salts that really

come from the sea. We thus have a salt stream running underground, from the mouth of a river to its source. And the earth would not contain salts if that salt stream did not flow back underground from river mouths to their source. Geologists studying the earth's interior will therefore always need to pay attention to the salt deposits found some way down beneath all river beds.

You see, gentlemen, [13] if there were no salt deposits in the soil, plant roots could not grow in it, for they grow precisely because they have, as it were, the salt of the earth for their food. Plants have the highest salt content down in the root; above ground they contain decreasing amounts, with least in the flowers. So we can ask why it is that our soil can produce plants. It is simply because there is in the earth a water circulation whose arteries, like arteries emerging from the heart and veins transporting blue blood back, go in one direction on the earth's surface, and go in the reverse direction carrying salt.

Why is it that the earth consists of a watery, salt body on the one hand and solid land on the other, and then of bodies of fresh water, rivers that flow through the landscape, and salt being brought back from the seas? Well, if you examine the salt water itself, sea water that contains a lot of salt, you will find that this salty sea water has little connection with the heavens and the cosmos. Just as our stomachs, for instance, have little connection with the outside world, except for what enters them, so the inner characteristic of the ocean has little connection with the heavens. But where rivers flow, where plants grow because of mineral deposits, but above all where waters flow, the land is very much connected with the heavens.

Looking at the matter like this, gentlemen, we go to our

mountain springs in a very different mood. We delight in the trickling, flowing springs with their wonderfully clear water, and so on. But this is not all. The springs are the earth's eyes. The earth does not look out into cosmic space via the oceans, for the sea is salty and this means that it inwardly resembles our stomach. The springs that flow with fresh water are open to the heavens, like our eyes which are also open to the outside world. So we can say that on land, where you have springs, the earth looks out far into the cosmos, as it were through the earth's sense organs. The body or innards of the earth, on the other hand, are the salty oceans. Of course it is not the same as in the human body; these are not organs complete in themselves that you can outline in their entirety. You could draw them but they are not wholly visible. But generally one can say that the earth has its innards in the ocean and its sense organs in the land. And everything that connects the earth with the cosmos comes from fresh water, while everything that gives the earth its innards comes from salt water.

I am going to demonstrate this now. I once told you that human and animal reproduction are connected with the heavens. I said that this is not only because the egg and the embryo in the mother's body develop only in this maternal body but also because influences enter from the universe. Because of such influences the egg develops its roundness ... this small egg is an image of the universe, for these influences come from all directions. This means that heaven is active on earth wherever reproduction is active. In the same way you see that the eye is a sphere, as I described the other day. It too has been created under the influence of the cosmos. If you look at the spleen it is not spherical but subject more to the sway of earthly influences ... In the egg the human and animal embryo initially develop as a sphere under the influence of the heavens.

Knowing this we have to say that fish are a special instance, for they do not live on land. They can at most gasp a little, but not live there, and must live in the sea. Because of this, fish have their own particular ways. They do not reach the places where the earth opens up to the cosmos. Fish therefore find it very difficult to develop their senses and especially their reproductive organs, for it is due to cosmic space that these can be situated internally. Fish therefore have to utilize the little light and warmth that enters the sea from the universe if they are able to reproduce and have sense organs. But nature takes care of many things. You can see this in goldfish which use the whole of their skin to receive the influence of light, and this makes them golden. Fish take every opportunity to snap up everything that falls into the water from the universe, and they always deposit their eggs in places where some light still penetrates ... what I am saying does not concern freshwater fish so much as sea fish. Sea fish always show that they are ready to utilize everything that reaches the salt water from the universe to enable them to reproduce.

Salmon are a strange exception however. They have a particular type of organization. Salmon must live in the sea to develop proper muscles. They need earth influences to feed properly and develop muscles, and these earth influences are mainly in the sea salt. Salmon must live in the salt of the sea in order to develop strong muscles. But they cannot reproduce if they live in the sea because they are constituted in such a way that the sea water closes them off entirely from the universe. Salmon would have died out long ago if they had to reproduce in the sea. They are an exception. As they gain their strength in the sea—where they develop their muscle—

they are fairly blind and unable to reproduce. Their reproductive organs and their sense organs grow weak and dull. But salmon grow big in the sea. Now to avoid dying out—and we can see this if we consider the salmon in the North Sea and in the Atlantic—they migrate up the Rhine year after year. This is why they are called Rhine salmon. But the Rhine makes salmon leap; they lose their muscles. The size to which they have grown in the salty sea is lost in the Rhine; they get very slender and lose some of their muscle. Their sense organs and above all their reproductive organs, male and female, develop to a great degree, and the salmon can reproduce in the Rhine. The salmon must thus migrate from the salty sea to the freshwater Rhine every year in order to reproduce. They have to grow lean because fresh water does not help their muscles develop. Then the old ones which are still living and the young ones that have arrived all migrate back to the sea to lose their slenderness and gain in size . . .

We may say that where the earth is salty it acts with earth forces. It acts on the organs that have been developed out of earth principles. Our own muscles are developed out of earth principles when we move in the field of gravity. Gravity is the earth principle. The earth influences everything that is muscular and bony. It gives us its salt and thereby we develop strong bones and muscles. But this salt from the earth does not aid development of our sense and reproductive organs, which would wither in this process. They must, instead, always come under the influence of forces from beyond the earth, influences from the cosmos. And the salmon show this, making a distinction between salt and fresh water. They enter salt water to fatten up, to absorb earth influences, and enter fresh water to be able to reproduce, to take in heavenly influences.

So we can say that the earth has a kind of circulation also when it comes to animals, like the salmon for instance. Salmon feel driven to move to and fro between the sea and the river. The whole shoal of salmon goes back and forth. Looking at salmon we can see how all life is in motion on earth.

Seeing this as we study salmon we can also gain an idea of something else, a marvellous spectacle continually repeated—the migration of birds. They move to and fro in the air in a similar way to the salmon in water ... except that salmon move back and forth between salt and fresh water while the birds in the air move to and fro between the colder and warmer regions which they need. If you understand the migration of salmon you also have an idea of the migration of birds. It all has to do with the fact that birds must go south to find the right temperature conditions on earth; they too develop their muscles. Then they need to return to the purer air of the north to absorb the influences that come from the cosmos, where they develop their reproductive organs. These animals need the *whole* earth. Only the mammals, higher animals and human beings, have grown more independent of the earth, somewhat more emancipated from it.

But nevertheless we can find traces of such things in our own constitution. In fact we human beings are really always two people ...—a right side and a left. The right side differs enormously from the left. I think very few of you sitting here before me are able to write with the left hand; mostly people write with the right. But the part of the nervous system which is connected with speech, for instance, is located in the left side of the brain. There you have marked convolutions, which do not exist in the matching area on the right. In the

case of left-handed people the opposite is true ... And likewise there are differences elsewhere in the body. The heart
lies more to the left, the stomach to the left and the liver to the
right. Even generally symmetrical organs are not entirely so.
The lung has two lobes on the left and three on the right. The
right thus differs greatly from the left in human beings. Why?
Let's start with something simple. We don't usually start to
write with the left but with the right hand. This is an activity
that depends more on the etheric body.[14] The physical body
has more weight, is more developed on the left, while the
etheric body is more developed on the right. Our left side
develops two lung lobes while the right, being more active,
develops three. People are more physical and earth-related
on the left and more etheric and cosmos-related on the
right ...

We see the world's secrets strangely revealed everywhere.
Imagine this is the surface of the sea and beneath it is the salty
sea water with all kinds of other substances in it. Now there
are some fish that are very oddly constituted and are greatly
inclined towards earth forces while all other fish really snap
up everything they can that enters into the water through
light and air. Having no lungs fish cannot breathe in the air
itself; but they absorb through their gills anything that enters
the water via air and light. There is one fish however—larger
species are called halibut, smaller ones plaice or sole—and
they are very nutritious, in fact contain the most nutrients of
all fish. This immediately shows they are inclined towards the
earth, for nutrients come from the earth. Our halibut is really

a devotee of the earth! So what can we expect of these fish? We can expect them to outwardly embody their deep connection with the earth. And they do. They lie so much on one side that it turns pale, white. And they lie so much on that one side that the head turns round and the eyes end up on the other side. A flatfish therefore looks like this from underneath: it is quite flat and white. And on the other side, seen from above, both eyes are on one side. The head has turned round because the fish is, as it were, always lying on its left side. The left side becomes the nutrient side, is pale and white. The other side takes its colour from the sky etc., turning bluish, brownish, and the eyes actually turn away from the nutrient side, with the head turning round. A flatfish like this is completely one-sided with its eyes and all organs on one side; the other side is flat and pale . . .

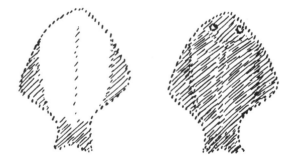

Human beings have emancipated themselves more from the earth than the halibut, but you might nevertheless find someone with a strange disorder, who sees slightly better with one of his eyes than the other. If this is not something he was born with we may find that he invariably lies on the other side to sleep. The earth forces frequently influence the side we lie on; the eye on that side grows a bit weaker, has weaker vision. The effect is not as powerful as in the halibut, but there is a little of it. The eye facing outwards towards the heavens, being turned away from the earth, grows a little stronger. You see, such strange connections exist. In one way or another nature will show us the forces it works with...

And the earth itself, what does it do? Well, gentlemen, if we only had salty oceans the earth would long since have perished, being unable to sustain itself. It does not only have salty water, though, but also fresh water, and this fresh water receives the power of procreation from the heavens. The salty sea cannot draw from cosmic space the element that continually refreshes the earth. If you go to a spring and see the trickle of marvellously pure water, you will find a lovely fresh smell surrounding it. That freshness around the spring also refreshes the whole living earth. It is at such places that the earth opens to the heavens as though through eyes and sense organs. And we can see that creatures such as salmon seek this out... In fact the springs are like the flatfish—they are the places on earth where the earth turns upwards to the light...

If one pays no attention to these things one really cannot understand life on earth at all. It is really true to say that the sea opens up to the heavens everywhere through the flatfish. The flatfish are proof that the sea thirsts for the heavens, for its salt content turns it away from the heavens. We can say that flatfish give expression to the sea's thirst for light and air.

Looking at our own circulation we find that we have subtle sense organs, organs of touch, in the places where we get more salty, where the muscles are. There human beings also open up to the external world—not in the way they do through the eyes, where they open directly to light. Those are the places, we might say, that correspond to the flatfish in the sea... Just as we get dextrous by making good use of our organs of touch, so flatfish grow dextrous by opening up to the heavens... Flatfish settle in shallower places by the shore. They push their way into the sandy bottom, using their mouths to cover themselves with a little sand, and then they stir the sand up to make a fine cloud or veil, fine enough for a fish to swim through. So fish and crabs come along and do not notice the flatfish—and suddenly, as they move past, the flatfish snaps them up. It does so in an extraordinarily clever way. But this can of course only be done by a creature that finds a subtle way to connect with the powers of the cosmos and the universe.

On the one hand, therefore, such a creature has developed its physical body, and on the other it develops a particularly strong etheric body. We can see from such things that everything which we likewise have in the form of mental and spiritual capacities does not derive from earth forces. Earth forces make us muscular, give us salts; while the powers of the cosmos really endow us with the capacities which are then both powers of procreation and powers of mind and spirit, that make us intelligent.

In fact we ourselves are really a small earth. As I have often said, we consist of 90 per cent water. So we are really also fish, for our solid constituents—floating in this water—account for only 10 per cent of us. Basically we are fish swimming in our own water. Modern science acknowledges that we are in a certain sense a small ocean ... but we also have freshwater currents, outside of our muscles and bones. In the muscles and bones, in contrast we have the same salt deposits as the ocean. We are definitely a small earth globe in this respect, with our salty sea inside us.

If someone develops in such a way that his fluids, his

freshwater currents, get too strong—this can easily happen in children when the mother's milk has insufficient salts in it—he or she gets rickets. Getting too much salt a person becomes too much sea; his bones grow brittle and his muscles clumsy and awkward. There always has to be the right balance between ingesting salt and the constituents found in other foods.

What things are there in other foods? . . . Plants have salts in their roots. But when the plant grows out of the soil it grows more and more towards flowering. The flower develops beautiful colours because it takes in light. Up there in the flower the plant absorbs light while in the root it takes in salts. Out there the plant becomes a bearer of light, down there a bearer of salts. Down there it becomes similar to the oceans of the earth while up above it becomes related to the heavens. The root is rich in salts, the flower in light . . . We may say therefore that we need light for the organs of the body that contain the freshwater currents, as it were; we need the principle which the plants give us when they move towards the light. For our bones and muscles, on the other hand, for the parts which need to be saltier, we need salt and the solid parts in our foods. And the balance between them must be right . . .

[The earth] likewise feeds itself through a continual exchange of substances, for the earth principle is all the time rising up in mists and vapours. And you know that rainwater which falls is distilled—pure water with nothing in it. But the earth feeds itself in a subtle way, from the heavens . . . feeds on the subtle forms of matter that are present everywhere in the universe. It is feeding all the time but we do not notice it because it feeds in such a subtle way. But you see, someone who looks at a human being in a rough and ready way may not notice that he is taking in oxygen all the time. In the same way we do not notice that the earth is continually absorbing nutrients from cosmic space . . .

13. A Water Sphere

Extract from a lecture given in Dornach on 28 October 1923

The silent fish is wholly immersed in the earth's sphere of waters. The croaking frog, by contrast, as amphibian, has half emerged from this enveloping sphere. These simple, self-evident facts form the basis upon which Steiner here speaks again of 'etheric' and 'astral': the first is manifest in the earth's living 'body of waters' and the second, connected with water's transition to air, is embodied in a more inward experience of soul qualities and in vocal utterance. Steiner states here that the earth's astral nature is expressed in weather fluctuations, whose continual changes we can easily experience as parallel to the 'weather' of human feelings.

It is interesting to ponder on this subtle transition which the frog represents between one realm and form of life and another: between complete immersion in life processes alone and, as this life is translated onto dry land, emergence into distinct, vocalized qualities of sentience and soul.

Thus the fish ... feels itself as a physical vessel of water. It feels the water within itself as part and parcel of all the waters of the world. Fluid traverses it as it were, is everywhere, and in this wetness the fish at the same time experiences the ether.[15] Fishes cannot speak but if they could, and could say what they feel, they would say: 'I am a vessel, but one which contains the all-pervading element of water, which is the bearer of the element of ether. I am really swimming in the ether.'... Thus the fish feels its life to be at one with the life of the whole earth. This is the peculiar thing about the fish: it feels its life as the life of the earth, and therefore takes an intimate part in everything that the earth experiences during the course of the year: the exhaling of the etheric forces in summer and the withdrawing and inhaling of etheric forces in winter.[16] The fish experiences something which breathes within the whole earth. The fish perceives the etheric element as the earth's breathing process...

The fish is the creature which takes part in quite an extraordinary way in the breathing life of the earth during the cycle of the year, because what is important for the fish is the element of life, the ether that surges out and in, drawing all other aspects of breathing with it.

It is different with the reptiles and with the amphibians— with the frogs for instance, which are remarkably character-istic in this respect. They are less connected with the ether in the cosmos and more with the astral...[17] I told you in regard to plants how the astrality of the cosmos touches the flower.[18] The frog is connected with this astrality, with what may be called the astral body of the earth, just as the fish is connected with the earth's ether body ... the frog lives in the general astrality of the earth, sharing particularly in the processes that occur in the cycle of the year when the earth brings its astrality into play in the evaporation of water and recon-densation. Here the materialistically minded person natu-rally says that the evaporation of water is caused by aerodynamic or, if you like, aero-mechanical forces of one kind or another: drops are formed, and when they become heavy enough they fall downwards. But this is like saying our blood circulates within us independently of the fact that we are living beings. In a similar way the earth's astral atmo-sphere lives in the cycle of water as it evaporates and recondenses. It is no fairy tale to say that the frogs—and other amphibians too to a lesser extent—live in this play of astrality which manifests in weather conditions, in meteorology. It is not just that frogs are used—as you know—in a very simple, basic way to foretell the weather, but they experience this astral play so wonderfully because their own astrality immerses them fully in the earth's astrality. The frog does not of course say 'I have a feeling', but it is simply the bearer of feelings that the earth has in wet spells, in dry spells and so on. This is also why in certain weather conditions you have the more or less beautiful, or ugly, frogs' concerts. This is how the frogs express what they experience in conjunction with the earth's astral body. They don't actually croak unless they are moved to do so by what comes from the whole cosmos; they live with the astrality of the earth . . .

Part Four:

PLANT AND PLANET

14. Sense Organs of the Earth

Extract from a lecture given in Berlin on 8 December 1910

Plants are the sense organs—tongues, eyes and noses—of the earth. They sense and resonate with forces coming from the cosmos, connecting these with earthly matter. In human beings the senses can be elevated and transformed into spiritual senses—the sense of smell for instance acting as a physical 'model' for non-material discernment of moral qualities. In a similar way we can regard flowers and plants as 'tuning' to and embodying different qualities in the cosmic and earthly environment, and expressing these in their myriad different gestures. Here Steiner also introduces the whole subject of planetary influences on natural processes. There is no scope here to give further details, but the influence of the moon has long been recognized by many as having an effect on plants, and there is good reason to extend this to the subtler effects of planets. Much research has been done on this area by people such as Maria Thun[19] and Lawrence Edwards.[20]

Just as every stone, every lifeless body, shows its relationship to the earth by being able to fall onto the earth, where it encounters resistance, so every plant shows its relationship to the earth in the direction of its stem, which is always aligned to the centre of the earth. All plant stems would cross at the earth's centre if we extended them to that point. The earth draws from its centre all those radiating forces that allow the plants to arise...

What our senses are for us, the plants are for the organism of the earth. But what is perceiving, achieving consciousness here, is the world of spirit streaming down from the sun to the earth. This world of spirit would not be able to achieve consciousness if it did not possess the plants as its sense organs, mediating self-awareness just as our eyes, ears and nerves mediate our own self-awareness ...

The spiritual entities that belong to earth activity and sun activity perceive through the plants as their organs, and these entities direct their gaze as it were towards the centre of the earth through all the organs they need to unite them with it. Thus we can see behind the earth's covering of plants the spiritual beings that weave round the earth and possess their organs of perception in the plants.

If we study the leaf of a plant we can find that its outer surface is actually a composite of many small, lens-like structures.

These light organs can be compared to a kind of eye, but the plant itself does not see by means of them; rather, the sun being gazes through them to the earth being. These light organs mean that the leaves of a plant always tend to place themselves perpendicularly to sunlight.

We have the plant's second main orientation in the way it surrenders itself to the sun's activity. The first orientation is that of the stem, through which plants reveal themselves as belonging to the earth's self-awareness; the second orientation is the one through which the plants express the earth's surrender to the activity of sun beings.

Thus we look to mother earth as to our great nourishing mother. In the earth's plant cover we have the physiognomy of the plant spirit, and this can give us the sense that ... we are gazing into the soul of the earth—just as we gaze into the eyes of another person—if we understand how its soul is manifest in the blossoms and leaves of the plant world.

Extract from a lecture given in Dornach on 9 August 1924

When you pick a violet you really only pick the solid part of it, and observe this solid part. But in fact the violet consists of more than this. What the violet really is, is enshrined in but not identical with this solid part. One can say that the real violet, which emits fragrance, is really a vapour existing within the petals and other parts of the flower—in the same way that you stand there in your shoes and boots . . . A being with a very delicate sense of smell would actually adapt its nature and being to the way it smells the universe.

Such beings do exist. There are beings that actually smell the universe, and these are the plants. They smell the universe and adapt themselves accordingly. What does the violet do? It is really all nose, a very, very delicate nose. The violet is beautifully aware of what streams down from Mercury, and it forms its scent-body and fragrance accordingly, while the asafoetida has a delicate perception of what streams from Saturn, and forms its vapour body accordingly, thus acquiring an offensive odour. And so it is that every kind of plant perceives smells that emanate from the planetary world.

But what about plants that have no fragrance? Why have they no scent? As a matter of fact, to sensitive noses all plants do have a certain scent—or at least what can be called a refreshing aroma—and this has a very strong effect upon them. This refreshing fragrance comes from the sun. A large number of plants are only receptive to this sun smell. But various plants, like the violet or asafoetida, are receptive to planetary influences; these are the sweet-smelling or bad-smelling plants.

And so when we smell a violet we can say that it is really all nose—but a delicate nose inhaling the cosmic scent of Mercury... Suppose you are walking through an avenue of horse chestnuts or of linden blossoms. They both have such perfume because their flowers are sensitive noses for everything that streams into the universe from Venus. And so the fragrances of heaven come to us through the plants...

We can say that the plants are the earth's delicate organs of smell. And the human nose, gentlemen, is really a coarse plant. It grows out of us like a kind of blossom, but has become coarse... It no longer has such delicate perception as the plants. These are pictures of course, but they are true...

So we can say that wherever we go in the plant kingdom we find the earth covered with noses—the plants... As a matter of fact, many blossoms look like a human nose. There are indeed plants—the snapdragons and Labiatae—which look just like a nose...

It might well be said that the human being is a poor creature; he has a nose for smelling but he can't smell much because his nose has grown too coarse, whereas the blossoms of the plant can smell the whole universe. The leaves of the plant can be compared to the human tongue; they can taste the world. The roots of plants can be compared to the organ in us which looks at and perceives things—our eyes—but in us it's a weak organ. Poor human being! He has everything that natural beings have, but in him it has grown more feeble.

15. Carbon and Oxygen

Extract from a lecture given in Dornach on
23 September 1922

Steiner is constantly aware of the symbiosis between different creatures and kingdoms of nature, and of the self-regulating wisdom of the planet and its interacting chemical substances. Here he looks at the relationship between plants and animals, and, long before destruction of the rainforest, hints at the disastrous effect cutting down forests would have.

Animal life would soon be in a bad state if all nature behaved as 'indecently' as human beings and animals who pollute the air. If all forms of life did the same, the earth would long since have reached a condition where nothing could live any longer, and the entire earth would be nothing but a cemetery. It is a good thing that the plants do not behave so indecently, but do the opposite. Whereas we and the animals inhale oxygen and poison the air with exhaled carbon dioxide, the plants inhale carbon dioxide, retain the carbon and release the oxygen. Due to the existence of plants, especially of forests, life on earth can continue. If there were no forests, or if huge corporations were to cut down the trees, as they are already doing to some extent, life would become much less healthy. It is vital to understand that we need the forests. If we are merely interested in the lumber and cut down trees, we gradually make life on earth impossible

Extract from a lecture given in Dornach on 31 July 1924

Actually, to be able to live on this earth the human being needs the plants. But now this is the amazing fact: the plants could not live on the earth either if human beings were not here! So, gentlemen, we reach the interesting fact—and we must grasp it quite clearly—that of all things the two most essential for human life are the green sap in the green leaves and blood. The green in the sap of a plant is called chlorophyll. Chlorophyll is contained in the green leaf. And the other essential thing is blood.

Now this brings us to something very remarkable.

Think how you breathe; that is also a way of taking in nourishment. You take oxygen in from the air; you breathe it in. But there is carbon spread through your entire body. If you go down into the earth where there are coal deposits, you've got black coal. When you sharpen a pencil, you've got graphite. Coal and graphite: they're both carbon. Your whole body is made of carbon (as well as other substances). Carbon is formed in the human body. You could say, a person is just a heap of black coal! But you could also say something else. Because—remember the most expensive thing in the world? A diamond—and that's made of carbon; it just has a different form. And so, if you like the sound of it better, you could say you're made of shining diamonds. The black carbon, that graphite in the pencil, and the diamonds: they are all the same substance. If some day the coal that is dug out of the earth can by some process be made transparent, you'll have diamonds. So we have diamonds hidden in our body. Or we are a coalfield! But now when oxygen combines with carbon in the blood, you have carbon dioxide. And you know carbon dioxide quite well. You only have to think of Seltzer water with the bubbles in it—they are the carbon dioxide. It is a gas. So one can have this picture: a human being inhales oxygen from the air, the oxygen spreads all through his blood; in his blood he has carbon, and he exhales carbon dioxide. You breathe oxygen in, you breathe carbon dioxide out.

In the course of the earth's evolution, gentlemen, which I have recently been describing to you, everything would long ago have been poisoned by the carbon dioxide coming from the human beings and animals. For this evolution has been going on for a long time. As you can see, the human kingdom or animal kingdom could never have existed on the earth unless plants had had a very different character from those kingdoms. Plants do not take in oxygen; they take in the carbon dioxide that human beings and animals exhale. Plants are just as greedy for the carbon dioxide as human beings are for oxygen. Now if we look at a plant—root, stem, leaves,

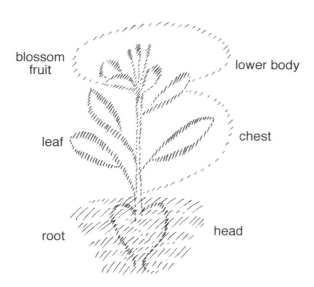

blossoms—the plant absorbs carbon dioxide in every part of it. And now the carbon in the carbon dioxide is deposited in the plant, and the oxygen is breathed out by the plant. Human beings and animals get it back again. The human being gives out carbon dioxide and kills everything; the plant keeps back the carbon, releases the oxygen and brings everything to life again. And the plant could do nothing with the carbon dioxide if it did not have its green sap, the chlorophyll. This green sap of the plant, gentlemen, is a magician. It holds the carbon back inside the plant and lets the oxygen go free. Our blood combines oxygen with carbon; the green plant-sap separates the carbon again from the carbon dioxide and sets the oxygen free. Think what an excellent arrangement nature has made, that plants and animals and human beings should complement one another in this way! They complement one another perfectly.

16. The Purified Longing of Flowers

Extract from a lecture given in Dornach on
10 November 1923

To delicate observation, the plants reflect our own nature back to us, in the tension between the 'root' of earthly comfort and the 'flower' of yearning for non-material realms. This might seem poetic fantasy, but Steiner means this in very tangible ways: we are intimately connected with the plant world, and it offers us true images of our moral nature. To some this might appear to be straying from the discipline of ecology, but as we have seen throughout this volume, Steiner believes that developing our own powers of qualitative perception for the meaning of natural phenomena is vital for reconnecting us consciously with the natural world. The human being cannot be left out of the equation.

Let us look at the plant world. Truly, this plant world has something of manifold enchantment to us when we begin to contemplate the plant cover of the earth with the eye of spirit. We go out into a meadow or wood. We dig up, let us say, a plant with its root. If we bring spiritual perception to bear upon what we have dug up, we find something magically complex.

The root shows itself to be something that has become entirely earthly. Yes, a plant root—the coarser the more so—is really something terribly earthly. A root, especially a turnip root for instance, always reminds one of a particularly well-fed alderman, extremely smug and self-satisfied. It has absorbed the salts of the earth and feels a deep sense of gratification at having soaked up the earth. In the whole

realm of earth there is no more absolute expression of satisfaction than such a turnip root, embodying root nature.

On the other hand let us look at the flower. When we
observe a flower with the eyes of spirit we cannot help
experiencing it like our own soul when it cherishes the ten-
derest desires. Only look at a spring flower—a breath of
longing, the embodiment of a wish. And something
wonderful streams forth over the world of flowers that surrounds us if only our soul perception is delicate enough to
perceive it.

In spring we see the violet, or say the daffodil, the lily of the
valley, or some plant with yellow flowers—and we are seized
by a sense that such spring-flowering plants wish to tell us: 'O
human beings, how pure and innocent can be the desires
which you direct towards what is spiritual!' The nature of
spiritual desire, desire bathed, as it were, in the divine,
breathes from every spring flower.

And when the later flowers appear—let us go straight to the
other extreme, let us think of the autumn crocus—can we
behold the autumn crocus without a slight sense of shame?
Does it not warn us that our desires can be infiltrated with all
sorts of corruption? The autumn crocuses seems to whisper
to us from all sides: 'Consider the world of your desires, O
human being; how easily it can be corrupted.'

Looked at thus, the plant world is the mirror of human
conscience in external nature. Nothing more poetical can be
imagined than the thought of this voice of conscience, which
in us comes forth from a single point, distributed over the
many different kinds of flowers that speak to the soul through
the seasons of the year in the most manifold ways. The plant
world reveals itself as the outspread mirror of conscience if
we know how to look at it rightly.

If we bear this in mind it comes to be of special significance for us to look at the flowers and conceive how they really embody our longing for the light-filled spaces of the universe, how they literally grow upwards in order to send the desires of the earth streaming towards the light-filled spaces of the heavens; and how, on the other hand, the substantial root fetters the plant to the earth, continually wresting those celestial desires away from the plant, striving to transform them into earthly ease and satisfaction . . .

17. Plants and Elemental Nature Spirits

Extract from a lecture given in Vienna on 28 September 1923

In former times people felt the whole natural world not only to be alive but to be full of fleetingly perceived nature or elemental spirits of different kinds. Steiner wants us to return—but more consciously now—to a perception of such beings and the dynamic spirit at work in natural phenomena. This is a tall order for those of us brought up on a stern diet of natural 'facts'. But it represents at the same time an imaginative leap into the very life of nature, into the 'green fuse' which in Dylan Thomas's phrase 'drives the flower'. Schooling our environmental and ecological perception does not mean forsaking clear thought for fantasy, but it does involve getting much closer to nature than our abstract heads often allow us.

Someone who grows up in and enters into contemporary civilization observes the things of the outer world. He perceives them, forms abstract thoughts about them, possibly derives genuine pleasure from a lovely blossom or a majestic plant. And if he is at all imaginative he may even form a living inner picture of it. Yet he remains completely unaware of his relation to that world of which the plant, for example, forms a part. Just to speak of spirit, spirit and again spirit is far from enough to develop spiritual perception. What we need, instead, is to become aware of our real spiritual relationship to the things around us. When we observe a plant in the usual way we do not in the least sense the presence of an elemental being dwelling in it, of something spiritual. We do not dream that every plant harbours something which is not satisfied by us examining it and forming the kind of abstract mental images we are used to. For in every plant is concealed—as though enchanted—an elemental spiritual being. And only they properly observe a plant who realize that this outer loveliness is the sheath concealing an enchanted spiritual being—a relatively insignificant being, to be sure, in the great scale of cosmic interrelationships, but nevertheless a being intimately related to the human being.

We are really so closely linked to the world that we cannot take a step into nature without falling under the direct influence exercised on us by our intimate relationship with everything. And when we see a lily growing from seed to blossom we must vividly imagine—though not personified— that this lily awaits and requires something from us. While unfolding its leaves, and especially its blossom, this lily really expects something. The spirit of the lily (I have to use human language although it is not quite adequate to express inherent realities) says to itself as it were: 'People will pass by and look at me; and when a sufficient number of human eyes have directed their gaze at me, the spell of my enchantment will be broken, and I will be able to start on my journey into worlds of spirit.' You may naturally object that many lilies grow unseen by human eyes. Yes, but then the conditions are different, and such lilies find their release in a different way. The law that decrees that a particular lily's spell will be broken by human eyes arises at the first human glance upon it. It is a relationship between human being and lily which both enter into. These elemental beings are all around us, begging us not to look at flowers so abstractly nor form such abstract images of them, but rather to let our heart and mind enter into what lives as soul and spirit in the flowers, imploring us to break their spell of enchantment. Human life should really be engaged in continuously releasing from enchantment the elemental spirits imprisoned in minerals, plants and animals.[21]

An idea such as this can readily be sensed in its abundant beauty. But when we grasp it in its full spiritual significance we can also feel the responsibility we thereby incur towards the whole cosmos. At the present epoch of civilization— when we are developing human freedom—our attitude towards the flowers is mere sipping at what we should really be drinking. We sip by forming concepts and ideas whereas we should really drink deeply by uniting, through our heartfelt awareness, with the elemental spirits of the things and beings that surround us.

As I said, we do not need to consider the lilies never seen by human eyes, but must concern ourselves with those that are seen, because they require a relationship with our heartfelt human awareness. An effect proceeds from the lily; and diverse, mighty and magnificent indeed are the spiritual effects that continually approach us from natural things when we walk amongst them. Those who have insight into such things continually perceive the diversity and grandeur of all that streams out to them from nature's elemental spirituality. It flows out and into them, streaming continually towards them as a supersensible spirituality poured out over external nature, which is a mirror of divine spiritual realms.

Extract from a lecture given in Dornach on
2 November 1923

Earth, water, air and fire are not just intellectual categories but are infused with actual beings. This is no more far-fetched, perhaps, than to consider—as modern scientists do—that matter itself is not solid at all, but composed of dynamically moving atoms.[22] *The beings Steiner describes, though, are not just in movement but have highly differentiated qualities, functions and sympathies, and are closely connected with the life of plants and insects. Allowing ourselves to imaginatively enter this vibrant panorama of living beings is at the same time a way to train perception of nature's subtlest energies and processes.*

When spiritual vision turns to the plant world we are immediately led to a whole host of beings which were known and recognized in ancient times of instinctive clairvoyance, but which were afterwards forgotten and today remain only as names used, perhaps, in poetry, to which contemporary people ascribe no reality. To the degree, however, to which we deny reality to the beings that flit so busily around the plants, we lose understanding of the plant world . . .

Plants send down their roots into the ground. Anyone who can observe what they really send down and can perceive the roots with spiritual vision (for this is necessary) sees how the root is everywhere surrounded by the activities of elemental nature spirits. And these elemental spirits, which an ancient clairvoyant perception called 'gnomes', and which we might call root spirits, can actually be studied through imagination and inspiration,[23] just as human life and animal life can be studied in the physical world . . .

The root spirits are very special earth folk, invisible at first to outer view, but so much the more visible in their effects; no root could develop, in fact, if it were not for what is mediated between the root and the earth by these remarkable beings, which bring the mineral element of the earth into flux in order to conduct it to the roots of plants.

These root spirits, present everywhere in the earth, get a very particular sense of well-being from rocks and metal ores... They are filled with an inner spirituality that we can only compare to that of the human eye or ear. For these roots spirits are wholly sense perception in their spiritual nature... They are entirely sense, which is at the same time intellect that not only sees and hears but immediately grasps what is seen...

The plant gathers the secrets of the universe and sends them into the ground, and the gnomes absorb these secrets into themselves from what percolates down to them spiritually through the plants. And because the gnomes, particularly from autumn on and through winter, in their migrations through ore and rock, bear with them what has percolated down to them through the plants, they are the beings within the earth which bear the ideas of the whole universe on their streaming, wandering journey through the earth.

We look out into the wide world. The world has been built of the spirit of the universe; it embodies and reveals the ideas immanent in the universe, in the spirit of the universe. Through the plants, which to them are the same as rays of light are to us, the gnomes take in the ideas of the universe and carry them in full consciousness from metal to metal, from rock to rock within the earth. These gnomes have immediate understanding of what they see ... they are the epitome of intellect... but an intellect so universal that they scorn human reason as something imperfect... The thoughts are already there for them. The ideas flow through the plants. Why, they think, don't people stick their noses into the earth, down to

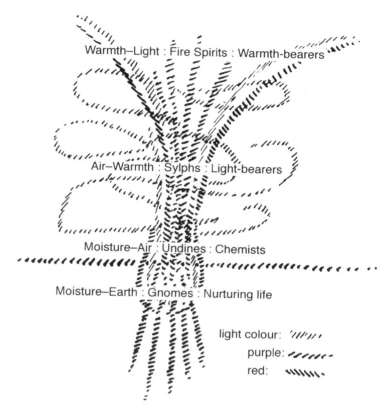

Warmth–Light : Fire Spirits : Warmth-bearers

Air–Warmth : Sylphs : Light-bearers

Moisture–Air : Undines : Chemists

Moisture–Earth : Gnomes : Nurturing life

light colour:
purple:
red:

the depths of the plant roots, and let what the sun says to the plants percolate down into their noses? Then they would know something! . . .

Thus the gnomes are actually the bearers of the ideas of the universe, of the cosmos, inside the earth. But for the earth itself they have no liking at all. They flit about in the earth with cosmic ideas, but they actually dislike what is earthly. This is something from which they would like to escape . . .

The gnomes are really the element within the earth that represents the extraterrestrial, because they must continually avoid growing together with the earthly. And it is from this feeling of dislike, of antipathy towards what is earthly, that the gnomes acquire the power to drive the plants up from the earth towards the heavens. With the fundamental force of their being they unceasingly thrust away from what is earthly, which determines the upward direction of plant growth . . .

Once the plant has grown upwards and left the realm of the root spirits, it passes from the moist element of earth into the sphere of moist air, and develops what comes to outer physical form in the leaves. Other beings are at work here in everything that goes on in the leaves—water spirits, elemental spirits of the watery element, to which an earlier instinctive clairvoyance gave the name of undines, among others. Just as we found gnomes flitting busily around the roots of plants, we see close to the surface of the soil these water beings, these elemental beings of water, or undines, who observe with pleasure the upward-striving growth that the gnomes have produced.

These undine beings differ in their inner nature from the gnomes. They cannot turn outwards towards the universe like a spiritual sense organ. They can only yield themselves up to the movement and activity of the whole cosmos in the element of air and moisture, and they therefore do not have the clarity of perception and intellect of the gnomes. They dream incessantly, these undines, but their dream is at the same time their own form. They do not hate the earth as intensely as the gnomes, but they have a sensitivity for what is earthly. They live in the etheric element of water,[24] swimming and floating in it . . .

In dreaming their own existence they bind and release, bind and separate the substances of the air, which in a mysterious way they introduce into the leaves. They take these substances to the plants that the gnomes have thrust upwards. The plants would wither at this point if it were not for the undines approaching from all sides. As they move around the plants in their dreamlike consciousness they prove to be what one can only call universal chemists . . . This undine dream is a universal chemist, binding and separating substances in the plant world, starting from the leaf . . . The undines wish to stay in a state of flux and metamorphosis, a state of endless change and mutation. But in this state of changeability, in which they dream of the stars and the sun, of light and heat, they become the chemists who now, starting from the leaf, continue with the further development of the plant form that was thrust upwards by the gnomes . . .

The plant now enters another, higher domain, that of the elementals living in air and warmth, just as the gnomes live in earth and moisture and the undines in air and moisture. In the element of air and warmth live the beings which a former clairvoyant faculty called sylphs. Because air is everywhere imbued with light, these sylphs living in air and warmth press towards the light and become related to it. They are particularly susceptible to more delicate but widespread movements and currents in the atmosphere.

When in autumn you see a flock of swallows, which produce vibrations in a body of air as they fly along, creating a current of air, this moving current—and this holds good for every bird—is something the sylphs can hear. Cosmic music is what they hear from it . . . The sylphs, which experience existence more or less in a state of sleep, feel most in their element, most at home, where birds are winging through the air. If a sylph is obliged to flit through the air devoid of birds, it feels as though it had lost itself . . .

Thus we behold the deepest sympathy between the sylphs

and the bird world. The gnomes hate the amphibian world, the undine is sensitive to fish, seeks to avoid them and feels a kind of horror of them, but the sylph is attracted towards birds and has a sense of well-being when it can waft towards their feathered flight in the floating air filled with sound... Their task is to lovingly convey light to the plant. Just as the undine is the plant's chemist, the sylph pervades the plant with light... The light, that is to say the power of the sylphs in the plant, works on the chemical forces induced in the plant by the undines, so that an interplay arises between the sylph's light and the undine's chemistry...

After it has passed through the sphere of the sylphs, the plant enters that of the elemental fire spirits inhabiting the element of heat and light... Just as the sylphs gather up and concentrate light in the plant, so the fire spirits gather warmth and bear it into a plant's blossom.

Undines carry the action of chemical ether into the plants, sylphs the action of light ether into the flowers. And the pollen provides what may be called little airships that enable the fire spirits to bear warmth into the seed. Everywhere warmth is gathered with the help of the stamens, and carried by means of the pollen from the anthers to the seeds in the carpel. And what is formed here in the carpel in its entirety is the male element that comes from the cosmos.

For plants the earth is the mother, the heavens the father... It is a colossal error to believe that the maternal principle of the plant is in the carpel. This is in fact the male principle drawn forth from the universe with the help of the fire spirits. The maternal element comes from the plant's cambium, lying between bark and wood ... and fertilization arises from the combined activity of the gnomes and fire spirits. The gnomes are in fact the spiritual midwives of plant reproduction...

Because people do not recognize what is spiritual, do not know that gnomes, undines, sylphs and fire spirits—which were formerly called salamanders—are actively involved in plant growth, there is a complete lack of clarity about the process of fertilization in the plant world. Fertilization itself does not actually take place up there, above the soil; the earth is the mother of the plant world, the heavens the father. This is the case in a quite literal sense. Plant fertilization takes place through the fact that gnomes take from fire spirits what these have borne into the carpel as concentrated cosmic warmth on the tiny airships of the anther pollen . . .

The sylphs experience their self, their ego, when they experience birds flying through the air. The fire spirits have this experience, but to an intensified degree, in relation to the butterfly world, and indeed the insect world as a whole. And it is these fire spirits which take the utmost delight in following the tracks of the insects' flight so that they convey warmth to the carpel . . . The fire spirits feel themselves intimately related to the butterfly world and the world of all insects in general. Everywhere they follow in the tracks of the insects as they flit from flower to flower.[25] And one really has the feeling when observing the flight of insects from flower to flower that each has a special aura which cannot be entirely attributed to the insect itself. Particularly the luminous, wonderfully radiant, shimmering aura of bees as they fly from flower to flower is unusually difficult to explain. And why? It is because the bee is continually accompanied by a fire spirit which feels so closely related to it that, for spiritual vision, the bee is surrounded by an aura endowed by a fire spirit . . .

If the earth is dense this is due to the antipathy by means of which the gnomes and undines maintain their form. When light and warmth descend to earth, this is at the same time an expression of the power of sympathy, the sustaining power of sylph love, which is borne through the air, and to the sustaining power of sacrifice of the fire spirits, which gives the power to descend to what is below. So we may say that, over the face of the earth, earth density, earth magnetism and earth gravity, in their upwardly striving aspect,[26] unite with the descending power of love and sacrifice. And in this interplay between downwards-streaming force of love and sacrifice and the upstreaming force of density, gravity and magnetism, in this interplay where the two streams meet, plant life develops on the surface of the earth . . .

Part Five:

PLANTS AND INSECTS

.

18. Nature's Wise Equilibrium

Extract from a lecture given in Koberwitz, Silesia, on
15 June 1924

*This key lecture from the 'Agriculture Course' stresses the
wonderful symbiosis between the plant, insect and animal kingdoms—how each is necessary to the other and performs a vital
service in the overall balance of nature. Steiner seems so far ahead
of his time in pleading for a rich diversity of interacting biosystems.*

*The terms 'astral' and 'etheric' which we have encountered
previously are here given a deeper complexity in relation to the
plant world. While, as stated earlier, the 'astral' realm is predominantly associated with more inward soul qualities, and the
'etheric' more with fluidic, rhythmic life processes, Steiner sees these
realms as interpenetrating and interacting. Thus the astral realm
'touches' plants from without, as it were, wherever a flower blossoms, and this is also of course where the world of flying insects
most interacts with the plants. To see bees buzzing around fragrant
flowers, for instance, is to become aware of a shimmering, moving,
intermediate realm where plant and creature meet. In this connection Steiner describes how we can develop our perception in
relation to smell, to increase our discernment of subtle qualities
revealed in the plant kingdom.*

*Whereas flowering trees are surrounded by this astrality at their
crown, their more mineralized roots dispel etheric life processes,
rendering the surrounding soil less imbued with life. We know that
plants, or even grass, generally do not thrive under trees. Yet, in
nature's wonderful balance, this offers favourable conditions for
the larva stage of insects.*

Insight into the interplay between all these different realms can show us how best to help a landscape regulate itself like a healthy organism.

Let us look at a tree with an eye to what it is within the totality of nature. If we look at it with understanding, the only parts we can consider plantlike are the thin, green stems which bear leaves, flowers and fruit. These shoots grow out of the tree in the same way as herbaceous plants grow out of the soil. As far as what is growing on its branches is concerned, the tree *is* the soil. It is heaped-up soil, soil that is simply in a more living condition than the soil in which our herbaceous plants and cereals are growing. To understand a tree we must consider, on the one hand, its thick trunk and also its limbs and branches. On the other hand there are the actual plants—the leaves and flowers that grow out of it. These plants are rooted in the twigs and branches of the tree just as other plants are rooted in the earth... One has to imagine that the roots of these 'plants' have been replaced by the tree's cambium layer. Although the cambium does not look like roots it is the layer that constantly produces new cells for continued growth just as if the herbaceous plant life above were growing from a root below. The cambium layer is the actual growth region; it can create new cells, whereas the other layers of the tree cannot do this.

Thus, in the tree, we can see that the solid, earthy element has in fact raised itself up, has grown up into the air, and why it therefore requires more internalized vitality than ordinary soil, which only has ordinary roots in it. Now we begin to understand the tree! We begin to understand it as a remarkable entity that exists in order to create a separation in the 'plants' that grow on it. It separates their stems and flowers and fruits from their roots, retaining only a more diffuse, etheric connection.

This is the macrocosmic approach we need to take in order to understand plant growth... The plants growing on the ground are surrounded by a hovering cloud of astrality, as I have described, but here in the treetops the astrality is far denser. Our trees are concentrations of astral substance; they are pronounced gatherers of astral substance.

This is actually the easiest area, I would like to say, in which to achieve a certain degree of higher development. If you make an effort you can easily develop esoteric perception here. You may not become clairvoyant but you can easily become clairsentient with regard to smell. Cultivate a sensitivity to the different fragrances that come from plants growing on the ground and those that come from orchards in bloom, or even from woodlands. Then you can tell whether the atmosphere around a plant is poor in astrality—as can be smelled around herbaceous plants growing on the ground— or rich in astrality, as can be experienced in the lovely scents wafting down from the treetops. If you cultivate your sense of smell, and can distinguish between the smell of plants growing near the ground and the smell of trees, you will have acquired clairsentience for astrality that is thinner in the first case and denser in the second...

In order to see where this leads we need to ask what exists as the counterforce to the astrality around the tree brought about by these 'parasitic' growths upon it.[27] What does the cambium actually do?

The tree makes the spiritual atmosphere around itself richer in astrality. What happens then when something resembling a herbaceous plant grows up there in the tree?

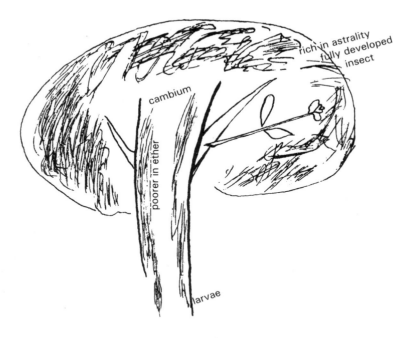

The tree has a certain inner vitality or 'ethericity', a certain intensity of life; but the cambium acts to damp down this vitality to a more mineral level. In other words, while a rich astrality arises around and outside the tree, the effect of the cambium is to impoverish the etheric forces within it. In comparison to herbaceous plants, trees are inwardly poorer in etheric force . . . and this in turn influences the trees' roots, which become much more mineralized than the roots of herbaceous plants. And, because their roots are more mineralized, these dispel some of the etheric force from the soil around them. The soil around trees is therefore less alive than around herbaceous plants. It is important to keep this clearly in mind.

A phenomenon like this always has a deeper significance within the whole balance of nature. If we look around we can find the significance of the astral richness around a tree's crown, and the etheric poverty around its roots. The rich astrality wafting through the trees provides the milieu for fully developed insects. And the etheric poverty below— which naturally extends through the tree since ... spiritual things always extend their influence over a totality—this etheric impoverishment affects the insect larvae. If there were no trees on earth there would not be any insects either. Trees make it possible for them to exist. The insects fluttering around the above-ground parts of the trees, and all through the forest, depend on the forest for their life; and their larvae too are alive because the forest is there.

This is a further indication of the intimate relationship that exists between everything rootlike and the underground animal world. Trees are the best example of what I've just explained; that is where it is most evident. But what is so clear and striking in the case of trees is actually present in varying degrees in all plants. Every plant has a certain tendency to become treelike. In every plant the root and its surroundings try to release etheric forces, while everything that grows upwards tries to attract and condense the astrality. The desire to become treelike is actually present in every plant. Thus every plant has the same relationship to the insect world that I described as being particularly characteristic of trees. But in addition, this relationship to insects widens out to include the animal kingdom as a whole. In times past the insect larvae, which are dependent for their survival on the presence of tree roots, evolved into other types of animals which they resemble. Such creatures spend their entire life in a kind of larval state, but they free themselves from the dependency on tree roots in order also to establish a connection with the roots of herbaceous plants.

As we shall now see, the remarkable thing about this is that certain subterranean animals—albeit only very distantly related to larvae—are able to regulate the etheric vitality in the soil when it increases too much. When the soil becomes too alive and exuberant, these underground creatures make sure that the excess vitality is released. Their special importance for the soil lies in their ability to serve as regulators or safety valves for underground vitality. These wonderful little creatures are the earthworms. It would be important to study the relationship of the earthworms to the soil because it is the earthworms which ensure that there is just enough ethericity left in it to support plant growth.

So down in the ground we find earthworms and other creatures vaguely reminiscent of larvae. And indeed in certain soils—which can be recognized just by sight—it would be good to encourage earthworm activity. Then you would see how beneficial this underground creature can be not only for vegetation but also, as we shall see, for animals.

Now again, there is a distant resemblance between the mature insects that fly and certain other animals, namely the birds. In the course of the earth's evolution something wonderful occurred between the insects and the birds. To put it pictorially, one day the insects said: 'We do not feel strong enough to cope with the astrality hovering around the trees, so we are going to leave most of it for you birds. Instead we will flutter around the other plants and make use of their desire to become treelike.' That is how a real division of labour arose in nature between the birds and the butterflies. These winged creatures work together in a quite wonderful way, sharing the work of distributing the astrality wherever it is needed in the air above the earth's surface. If you took away all the flying creatures this astrality would fail to fulfil its proper role, and you would notice a certain stunting of the vegetation. Winged animals and everything that grows upward into the air belong together; one cannot imagine one without the other. That's why on a farm we also need to have the insects and birds flying about. Farmers need to understand the importance of nurturing insect-life and bird-life properly, because everything in nature is interdependent—everything. This cannot be emphasized too often.

We need to keep these things vividly in mind because they are very important for our insight here. The right astralization of the air is brought about by the world of flying creatures, and this astrality interacts with wooded areas, which direct it in the right way, just as certain forces in our body direct our blood. The effect of a forest is felt over a very wide area, and in areas with no woods this function must be performed by something else. We must realize that in areas where fields and meadows alternate with woods, the vegetation is subject to quite different laws than in vast, treeless regions.

You can tell that some regions of the earth were heavily forested before human beings had anything to do with this—for in certain matters nature is still wiser than people are—and it's safe to assume that if forests are naturally present in a given area their presence has certain advantages for the herbaceous and grassy vegetation of surrounding farms. In such areas we should have the insight not to cut down all the forests but to take good care of them. However, since the earth is also slowly changing due to all kinds of climatic and cosmic influences, we should also have the courage—if we notice the vegetation on our farms is becoming stunted—to expand the wooded areas in our vicinity instead of merely doing all kinds of experiments on and with the fields. On the other hand, if we notice that plants are growing in a rampant vegetative way, but lack the strength to form seeds, we should take steps to clear certain areas in the woods . . .

If we trace these intimate relationships in nature in the right way we can also acquire insight into the nature of pests. Just as the coniferous forests have a particular relationship with birds, and the bushes an intimate relationship with animals,[28] so do all the fungi have an intimate relationship with lower forms of animal life, to bacteria and similar creatures, particularly harmful parasites. The harmful parasites go hand-in-hand with the fungi, and appear wherever the latter are present, causing plant diseases and abnormalities. But if, in addition to woodland, we also manage to have some wet meadows near the farm, these meadows will prove very helpful to it by providing a good soil for mushrooms. We should actively encourage mushrooms and toadstools to grow in these meadows. You will then experience the remarkable fact that if you have even a small area where mushrooms are growing, their relationship to the bacteria and other parasitic creatures will keep these creatures away from everything else. The mushrooms have a much stronger relationship to these creatures than the other plants do . . . it is quite possible to keep harmful microorganisms away from the farm simply by establishing some wet meadows.

The correct balance of woods, orchards, bushes and meadows—with their natural growth of fungi—is so essential to good farming that your farm will really be more successful, even if this means a slight reduction in your tillable acreage. There is no true economy in using so much of your land that all the things I've mentioned disappear. The resulting loss in quality will far outweigh the advantage of being able to cultivate a larger area at the expense of the other things . . .

19. Perfect Symbiosis: Flower and Butterfly

Extract from a lecture given in Dornach on 26 October 1923

The following two extracts continue with the theme of symbiosis between the plant and insect kingdoms, now in relation to the butterfly in particular. In his beautiful description Steiner shows us the close parallel between the 'freed' flower (the butterfly) and the 'tethered' butterfly (the plant). As ever, his view of the natural world is subtly different from Darwin's natural selection. The latter school of thought regards the extraordinary mutuality in nature as parallel adaptation for the benefit of each creature. As such it emphasizes the contest for survival—the 'selfish gene' in Dawkins's phrase. Such mutuality is central to Steiner's view too, but in his holistic perspective there is an underlying wisdom and love at work in the universe, in the mutually sustaining interdependence of everything. In this view, everything serves everything else. The 'microcosm' of each creature is thus like a cell in a multi-celled, cooperative organism.

Now investigate any place where the butterfly deposits its egg, and everywhere you will find that the egg is deposited in such a way that it cannot be withdrawn from the sun's influence... The butterfly never deposits its eggs where they cannot remain in some way or other connected with the sun. It is therefore wrong to say that the butterfly lays its eggs in the earthly domain. It lays its eggs in the sphere of the sun. The butterfly never descends as far as the earth. Wherever the sun is present in what is earthly the butterfly seeks out the place to deposit its eggs so that they remain entirely under the sun's influence. In no way do they fall under the sway of the earth.

Then, of course, a caterpillar emerges from this butterfly's egg. It remains under the influence of the sun but now comes under another influence as well. The caterpillar would be unable to crawl if it did not also fall under the influence of Mars . . .

Then the caterpillar becomes a chrysalis . . . The caterpillar is exposed to the light, follows the rays of light, spins, stops when it is dark, and then goes on spinning again. The whole cocoon is actually cosmic sunlight, sunlight interwoven with matter . . . But for this to happen the influence of Jupiter is needed . . .

Then, as you know, the butterfly emerges from the cocoon, from the chrysalis—the butterfly which is borne on the light and radiant with light . . . Here the sun comes under the influence of Saturn, and only in conjunction with this planet can it send its light into the air in such a way that the butterfly can shine in the radiance of its many and varied colours.

And thus when we behold the wonderful sea of fluttering butterflies in the air we must say that this is in truth no earthly creation but is born into the earth sphere from above . . .

Thus I might say that in the butterflies we must see creatures strewn down upon the earth by the sun and other aspects of our planetary system. The butterflies, the dragonflies and the insects in general are actually the gift of Saturn, Jupiter, Mars and the sun. And not a single insect could be produced by the earth, not so much as a flea, were it not for the fact that the planets and the sun bestow this gift upon the earth . . .

And what you have here in the butterfly under the influence of the extraterrestrial cosmos, this whole development from embryo to caterpillar, from chrysalis to butterfly—is something you can now find reflected in the plant. When the seed ... is entrusted to the earth—not now to the sun—the plant's root develops, the first thing to arise. And instead of the caterpillar emerging from the egg under the influences of forces which proceed from Mars, the leaf arises, emerging in a rising spiral. The leaf is the caterpillar which has fallen under the sway of what is earthly. When you see the creeping caterpillar you have, in upper regions, what corresponds below to the leaf of the plant. This latter develops out of what became root through the fact that the seed was transferred, as it were, from the sun sphere to the earthly domain.

Proceeding further upwards you get increasing contraction until, at the top, in the calyx, you have what corresponds to the chrysalis. And finally the 'butterfly' develops in the flower which is coloured just like the butterfly in the air. The circle is complete. Just as the butterfly lays its egg so the flower develops within itself the new seed for the future. So you see, we look up towards the butterfly and understand it to be the plant raised up into the air...

We can therefore contemplate two verses which give expression to a great secret of nature:

Behold the plant:
It is the butterfly
Fettered by the earth.

Behold the butterfly:
It is the plant
Freed by the cosmos

The plant—the butterfly fettered by the earth! The butterfly—the plant freed from the earth by the cosmos!

If one looks at a butterfly, or indeed any insect, from the stage of the egg to when it is fluttering away, it is the plant raised up into the air, fashioned in the air by the cosmos. If one looks at a plant it is the butterfly held in fetters below. The egg is claimed by the earth. The caterpillar is metamorphosed into leaf formation. The chrysalis formation is metamorphosed into what is contracted in the plant. And then the same principle that unfolds to produce the butterfly develops into the flower in the plant. Small wonder then that such an intimate relationship exists between the world of the butterflies, the insect world in general, and the world of the plants . . .

You see, one must really say that understanding of the world cannot come about through abstractions, for abstraction does not penetrate to full understanding. Cosmic activity is indeed the greatest of artists. The cosmos fashions everything according to laws which bring the deepest satisfaction to the artistic sense. And no one can understand the butterfly fettered to the earth unless he metamorphoses thoughts artistically. No one can understand how the plant's flower has been raised up into air by the light and cosmic forces to become butterfly unless, once again, he can bring abstract thoughts into dynamic, artistic movement. There is always something immensely uplifting about the deep inward connection between the different realms of nature.

It is a unique experience to see an insect poised on a plant and at the same time to see how astrality holds sway above the blossom. Here the plant is striving away from the earthly. The plant's longing for the heavenly holds sway above the iridescent petals of the flower. The plant cannot itself satisfy this longing. Thus there radiates towards it from the cosmos what is of the nature of the butterfly. In beholding this, the plant realizes the satisfaction of its own desires. And this is the wonderful relationship existing in the environment of the earth: that the longings of the plant world are assuaged in looking up to the insects, in particular the world of the butterflies. What the blossoming flower longs for, as it radiates its colour out into space, becomes for it something like known fulfilment when the butterfly approaches it with its shimmer of colours. Longing that makes warmth radiate outwards, satisfaction streaming in from the heavens—this is the interplay between the world of the flowering plants and the world of the butterflies...

Extract from a lecture given in Dornach on 19 October 1923

Passing from the more vegetative stage of the larva to the stillness, quasi-death and radical transformation of the pupa, we can see that the developing insect is, for a time, separating itself from vegetative life forces (the etheric) as it progresses towards the greater freedom and movement of the emerging butterfly. The interiority of the chrysalis seems to herald the more inward nature of the animal, and still more of the human being who can separate himself from his environment and develop an autonomous inner life.

As you know, the butterfly lays its egg, and from that egg a caterpillar emerges. The egg completely encloses and contains everything that later gives rise to the butterfly. The caterpillar emerges from the egg into the light-irradiated air. That is the environment into which the caterpillar emerges. The important thing to note is that the caterpillar really lives in the sunlit air.

This is something you can study when you're lying in bed at night and have lit your lamp, and a moth flies towards it and finds its death in the light. The effect of the light on the moth is such that it seeks its death. There you see how light acts on a living creature.

The caterpillar ... cannot reach the source of light, the sun, to cast itself into it, but would like to. It wants it just as much as the moth does which casts itself into the flame of your bedside candle and there meets its death in the physical flame. The caterpillar ... cannot throw itself into the sun, so its passage into heat, into light, is therefore a spiritual act for the caterpillar... The moth casts itself into the flame at one moment, giving the whole of its moth substance over to the light; the caterpillar gradually weaves its caterpillar substance into the light, pauses at night, weaves by day and spins and weaves a whole cocoon around itself. The cocoon, the threads of the cocoon, are what the caterpillar weaves out of its own substance as it spins on in the flood of sunlight. And so the caterpillar, once it has become a chrysalis, has woven around itself, out of its own substance, the sunbeams to which it has merely given physical substance. The caterpillar, sacrificing itself, casts itself into the sunlight and weaves around itself the threads of the sunbeams, following the direction in which they go at any given moment. If you look at a silkworm cocoon you are looking at woven sunlight, but sunlight given physical form from the substance of the silk-spinning caterpillar itself. The result is an enclosed space so that external sunlight has in a sense been overcome within.

You'll remember that when I described the Druid mysteries I spoke of the sunlight which enters the cromlech becoming inward. The sun, which previously exerted its physical power, causing the caterpillar to spin its own cocoon, now exerts power on what is inward and interior, and out of this creates the butterfly, which then emerges. Then the whole cycle begins again...

20. Insect Intelligence

Extract from a lecture given in Dornach on 5 January 1923

Intelligence is not just something we 'possess', located in our brains, but is a force permeating nature that can, for instance, be seen in the extraordinary wisdom of insect life. This idea of an intelligent universe or of intelligence manifesting in all phenomena is actually also central to the sense of the earth as a living, self-regulating organism that can be found in the works of James Lovelock or Arne Naess (founder of the 'deep ecology' movement).

If you look at a small beetle you can easily see that it has a small head. If you dissect the head of such a beetle—the burying beetle for instance—you discover nothing like a brain, which is supposed to be the thinking apparatus. Naturally the tiny beetle has no brain in this sense, but only a little bundle of nerves you might say. It does not even have the beginnings of a brain...

These burying beetles always lay their eggs, and maggots hatch from them that only later change into beetles. As soon as they have emerged from the eggs these tiny maggots require meat for their nourishment. They could not live without it. So what does the burying beetle do? It searches in the field for a dead mouse or bird or mole, and having discovered one—a dead mouse for example—it runs home again only to return not alone but with a number of other beetles. The beetles it has returned with all run around the mouse... first they dig the ground under the mouse and then all around it. The mouse gradually sinks deeper and deeper into the earth as they continue digging. They dig until the mouse finally falls into the ground. Then they fetch the females, who lay their eggs in it. Finally they cover the hole completely so that passers-by won't notice it...

It is unbelievably strange but true that only 10 or 12 beetles return with the one that makes the discovery, never 40 or 50. Only as many beetles return as are needed to do the work...

The person who first described the activity of these beetles wasn't a superstitious person but someone of sound judgement—the botanist Gleditsch ... he was involved in experimental work and once used toads in his experiments. These tests were intended for something completely different—you know that electricity was first discovered through work on a frog's thigh—and he needed to dry a dead toad ... he took it outside and pinned the dead toad to a small piece of wood to let the sun dry it quickly. After a while he returned to check it and found a number of beetles hard at work around it... They continued digging until the wood fell and the toad found a place in the ground; then the females came to lay their eggs in it. That done, the beetles covered the toad and the wood it was pinned to with earth. Now if a human being were to do that one would think he buried the stick to hide every trace. So you see, the burying beetles do exactly what an intelligent human being might do. Indeed, I am convinced that many people would be a good deal less skilful. You see, therefore, that what is called cleverness, or intelligence, is there without the beetles possessing it.

One might call this nonsense and say that it need not be regarded as intelligence ... since it is simply instinct. Actually I don't believe the word 'instinct' explains anything in this case ... It is applied to everything so that one doesn't have to think any more about it...

Now I'll tell you another anecdote that was told by a person of incontestable authority, one that has also been reported by others but above all by Darwin . . . he observed this activity in wasps, not beetles. Wasps have brains that are no larger than those of beetles. Their larvae also require meat as soon as they hatch. These wasps are weaker than beetles, even in groups, so they cannot deal with moles or dead toads but prefer smaller creatures that they can manage without help. This is why wasps gather little animals like flies for their young.

Darwin, who is considered the greatest scientist of the nineteenth century, observed a wasp that needed such an insect—a female wasp, heavy with eggs, looking for an insect into which to lay them. Finding a dead fly on the ground she tried to fly away with it, but this was too difficult for her. What did the wasp do? It bit off the fly's head and hind-quarters, and flew off with the thorax and wings which it could manage. The wasp could now fly without the fly's head and hindquarters. Darwin watched all this—a strong breeze was blowing and the wasp could not fly forwards because the fly's wings caught the wind. The two wings caught the wind and it could not get anywhere. So what did the wasp do, laden with the fly? It landed again on the ground, bit off the two wings and flew away with the fly's thorax without the wings.

In this case it is impossible to say that this is anything else but deliberate, since the wasp, after all, made a calculated allowance for the wind. It cannot be inherent instinct in the wasp to bite off the fly's wings . . . Here intelligence is at work.

Now you can see how scientists proceeded in the nineteenth century. I purposely mentioned Darwin here, who observed this. But what was his conclusion? Darwin said that everything we meet in the animal kingdom arises solely through heredity and natural selection.

To formulate theories, people simply suppress what they themselves know... Darwin was certainly a great man, and nobody has acknowledged his positive accomplishments more sympathetically than I. I have written all sorts of things in support of Darwin. But oddly enough we must realize that even those who have made significant contributions to science have suffered from the malady of having no eyes for the facts in front of them...

Now let us continue by considering other insects. In these matters one must study insects because they can illumine our subject particularly well; we can be quite sure in their case that they do not owe their intelligence to having a large brain... There are some insects which, when mature, feed only on plants... The strange thing is that their larvae, the maggots, require meat when they hatch. These insects therefore have the strange peculiarity that they are born with a completely different food preference from the one they later acquire. They convert to plant food only when fully developed... The mature insects seek out other insects, usually caterpillars, and lay their eggs on the backs of the latter. They themselves have no appetite for meat but they know that maggots requiring meat will hatch from their eggs, and lay their eggs in the body of a caterpillar or similar... Sometimes numerous eggs are deposited, filling the caterpillar's body, and from these the maggots hatch ... which can only survive on living flesh. Consider therefore that if a maggot were to destroy a vital organ in the host insect, thus causing its death, all the other maggots hatching out would die. These little creatures are so clever however that nothing is ever eaten in the living caterpillar except those parts it can survive without.

All vital organs are spared and the caterpillar remains alive. Regardless of how many eggs are deposited, only as much is consumed as ensures the host insect stays alive ...

Thus it is possible to say that while such insects do not possess intelligence since they have no apparatus for it—i.e. brains—intelligence is nevertheless working in what they do, and it must be admitted that intelligence is present. The creatures do not deliberate, which would require a brain, but their activities are informed by intelligence ...

You see, what works as intelligence through the human head is also at work everywhere ... even in insects a marvellous intelligence is at work. Picture the wonderful intelligence at work when the larvae that hatch inside the caterpillar's body do not feed immediately on its stomach. If they did, all the maggots would perish. Compared with the tactics employed by human beings during war, the intelligence governing the insect arouses respect and exposes the foolishness of human beings. In this regard human beings have no reason to claim sole possession of intelligence.

Now here is something else. You are all familiar with paper. You all know that the paper we have today was invented no earlier than four or five hundred years ago. Before this, parchment and all sorts of materials were used for writing. Civilized human beings discovered so-called rag paper just four or five centuries ago, and before this they wrote on leather and so on. How was paper discovered? People had to discover how to mix together certain substances in a specific way. Maybe you have visited a paper factory. At first the paper is in a liquid form and it is then solidified. It is produced in a purely artificial way by various chemical and mechanical means. You may also have seen a wasp's nest, which is built like this [sketches]. It is attached to something and formed so that the wasps can fly into it. It is grey, not white—but paper can be grey too—and this wasp's nest is real paper. A wasp's nest is chemically identical with paper—it is real paper.

But wasps have been building their nests for thousands and thousands of years, not just four or five hundred. You can see, therefore, that wasps manufactured paper long before humans. That's simply a fact: the wasps' nest is made of paper. If, thousands of years ago, people had been clever enough to examine the substance of a wasps' nest, they would have discovered paper then...

Naturally I could go on, not for hours but days, to speak of how intelligence pervades everything and is found everywhere. We simply accumulate this intelligence spread out through the world and put it to use. Owing to our well-developed brain we can put to our own use what permeates the world. Thanks to our brain we can utilize for our own benefit the intelligence contained in all things.

Our brain is not given us for the purpose of producing intelligence. It is sheer nonsense to believe that we produce intelligence. It is as stupid as saying: 'I went to the pond with a bucket to fetch water—and look, it contains water now. A minute ago there was none in the bucket, so the water must have materialized from its sides!' That's nonsense of course—the water came from the pond. Experts however point to the brain, which simply collects intelligence because it is in everything, like the water, and claim that intelligence emerges from it. This is as foolish as saying the bucket produces water. After all, intelligence is even present where there is no brain, just as the pond does not depend on the bucket. Intelligence exists everywhere and we can take hold of it...

21. The Sting of Life: Ants, Wasps, Bees

Extract from a lecture given in Dornach on
15 December 1923

In nature nothing takes without at the same time giving something back. The self-regulating wisdom of the whole continually redresses deficiencies and imbalances—in other words continually heals itself.

There is another type of ant that does the following. Somewhere on the ground it constructs a rather high mound; then it forms a circle surrounded by soil and burrows into the ground there. Sometimes this mound can come to resemble a volcano. Inside are the passageways that radiate into the surrounding area. Well, these ants then engage in a very unusual action. They bite and destroy all the grasses and plants that grow on the area they claim, with the exception of one type of grass.[29] Anything else they keep destroying. Sometimes they bite away and destroy everything, so that all that is left is the mound, and around it an area that looks as if it were paved. It appears so because soil becomes more compact as all living plants are removed from it. It becomes very smooth and begins to look like asphalt, only much lighter in colour.

Now these ants go out further into the surrounding area to find and bring back a specific grass, which they then plant. As soon as the wind blows other seeds into their cleared area and they begin to germinate, the ants quickly bite off whatever appears above ground and carry it away from the area they have prepared . . . Thus the ants lay claim to a patch of land and plant it only with what suits them. The grass they grow has a very different appearance when you compare it with the same grass growing elsewhere. Usually this grass grows in a loose soil, which is why it looks different. The soil prepared by the ants is very hard so that the grass growing there produces extremely hard seeds, hard as a pebble.

Yes, gentlemen, you can find such ant colonies, of what are called agricultural ants (*Atta malefaciens*) that tend the fields around them. This is what Darwin, who has studied them carefully, calls them . . . Then, when their crop is ready, the ants come out, bite off the portion above ground and carry it back into their mound . . . Everything that they can't use, which is attached to the seed, they bite off . . . they dump whatever they don't need and keep the pebble-hard seeds, some of which they break open with their extremely hard jaws and eat, and others which they use to sow their crop again. They really are farmers.

When you think about what is happening here you can discover that a new type of grass is actually being created! These seeds that are like pebble-hard rice kernels don't exist anywhere else. They are created by these ants . . . What is really happening here? Before we try to answer this question, let's look at this matter from another perspective. Let's examine wasps again. There we'll find, as I told you, creatures that lay their eggs in leaves or bark, out of which so-called gall apples are formed, from which young wasps will eventually emerge.

This can also happen differently. [Steiner describes wasps laying eggs in living caterpillars, see above pp. 119–20.]

This arrangement, that these wasp larvae simply don't bite into a part of the caterpillar that could cause it to die, is full of wisdom. Perhaps you have even seen this phenomenon, how the larvae emerge when they are mature enough. They crawl out once the caterpillar has served with its entire body as foster mother for the whole brood. They crawl out, develop into ichneumon flies [a type of wasp] and seek nourishment from flowers and similar plants. And then, when they are mature enough, they will in turn deposit their eggs into similar caterpillars.

Now you could say there is really something very intelligent in all of this. And indeed, as I've said, your astonishment will become greater the more you begin to carefully observe these things. You begin to marvel and then ask yourself what the connections are between all these things. Let's now get to the bottom of all this. First we tell ourselves that there are the flowers that grow from the soil. There are caterpillars present. Now insects come and gorge themselves on what they find available in the form of flowers and caterpillars; then they reproduce. This same story keeps repeating time and time again. It might seem as if the entire insect world could disappear and it would be no great loss for us human beings. When we look at bees we say that they produce honey for us, and beekeeping is therefore useful. Fine, but that is looking at the whole matter only from a human perspective. If it turns out that bees can be considered robbers that simply take nectar away from the flowers, and we can then use this honey for nourishment, even for curing diseases, the whole matter is thought very favourable from our point of view . . . But if one looked at things from the point of view of the flowers one might jump to the conclusion that this is simply robbery, with human beings as accessories to the crime . . .

People who know no better lament the fate of 'these poor flowers,' and these poor creatures, the caterpillars'. They think these terrible parasites devour them ... However this is not the case at all. If you come up close to a flower and see an insect, say a bee, sitting on it and sucking the flower's nectar, you have to ask what would happen to the plant if the bee, wasp or other insect did not come to the plant and remove its juice. This is a more difficult question than the one involving straightforward robbery. One must take a deep look into the entire ecology[30] of nature ...

You see, gentlemen ... these flowers absolutely need a chemical substance that also plays an important role in the human body. If you analyse the human body chemically, you'll find various substances, all continually undergoing changes. Everywhere, though, these substances are transformed into something that is always present in the human body, which it likewise needs—into formic acid.

If you go out to an anthill, collect ants and squeeze them, you'll obtain a juice. This juice contains formic acid and some alcohol. This is the juice in ants. But you too have this juice very thinly distributed throughout your body. Whatever you eat as long as you are alive will always be changed—not exclusively, since there are other substances in smaller quantities—to formic acid. It fills your entire body. Without sufficient formic acid you ... can fall ill with symptoms of gout or rheumatism, a condition in which the body creates too much uric acid and not enough formic acid.

So ants have in themselves the same thing that human beings need. But formic acid is, on the whole, something that is needed throughout nature. You won't be able to find any tree bark that does not contain some formic acid. You can find formic acid throughout the tree, just as you will throughout the human body. However, it is not only formic acid that is required there, but something related to it which is what wasps and also bees have in themselves, a chemical substance that they transform into bee poison. All these insects carry within them a certain chemical substance that is poisonous. If a bee stings you, the place will become inflamed; and the same if you're stung by a wasp, which some people react to quite badly ... and finally if an ant bites you, there will also be a slight inflammation, because the ant allows some formic acid to stream into the puncture. As stated, formic acid is present, in precisely the right dilution, in all living things.

Gentlemen, if there were no ants, bees or wasps—which produce these poisons—what would happen?... If you go out and see a bee sitting somewhere on a willow tree or on a flower, then instead of saying that the insect is simply robbing the flower and stealing its nectar you must realize that the flower is having such an enjoyable experience that it sends out its juices towards the place where the bee is sucking...

In this stream of flowing juice, while the bee is withdrawing something from the flower, bee poison also flows in the opposite direction, from the bee to the flower. And while the gall wasp is stinging, wasp poison likewise flows into the plant. And, in particular, when an ant crawls on a flower, even over the dead portions of it such as the bark, it allows formic acid to flow into it. When an ant crawls on a flower, flower juice combines with formic acid. And this is necessary. If it didn't happen, and if there were no bees, wasps and ants continually entering into contact with the world of flowers and nibbling at them, then the necessary formic acid and the other necessary substances would not flow towards these flowers, and after a certain period of time they would die out...

Understood in a very basic way, flowers are continually

getting sicker and sicker, and these little bees, wasps and ants continually play the role of doctor, bringing the flowers formic acid which they need to fully recuperate again. So they are not simply robbers, these bees, wasps and ants; at the same time they enable the flowers to stay alive.

And it is the same with the caterpillars. They would die out, would simply cease to exist after a certain period of time. Well, you might say, that wouldn't be such a great loss; this type of caterpillar would simply become extinct. But then you need to consider that the birds eat them, and so forth. All of nature is interrelated in this way. When we observe, for example, that ants penetrate everything with their formic acid, we have gained an insight into the inner workings of nature's ecosystem. This is truly something grand. Everywhere things are happening that are absolutely necessary for maintaining life and this world's continued existence . . .

Originating from anthills, formic acid penetrates right into the forest soil.

If you have the floor of a forest here and an anthill over here, it is like taking a glass of water and putting a drop of something into it, which immediately expands to fill the whole glass. If you put salt into it, all the water becomes salty. If you have an anthill here, then the formic acid seeps in similar fashion into the forest floor. The entire forest floor, which is dying off, becomes saturated with this formic acid . . . but it also penetrates the living plants . . .

The earth's soil, wherever things are dying off and mould is growing, is saturated with what the bees, wasps and ants give it. To be sure, bees give it only to living flowers, and wasps almost always to living plants. But ants also directly transmit formic acid to rotting or dead material, and by doing so they stimulate life to a certain extent, thus helping to maintain the life of the earth with all its decaying substance . . .

Let's return now to the agricultural ants that set up their little fields where they grow and tend their plants. It is true that we could not survive on the food they grow there. For if a human being were to try to eat these little rice kernels that are hard as pebbles he would, firstly, become strangely ill from ingesting too much formic acid, and secondly he would probably break a tooth or two and have to go to the dentist . . .

But the ants, or more accurately the entire colony, say to themselves: 'If we simply go out into the open fields and suck from plants the substance which we find present everywhere, we will not be able to create within us enough formic acid, and as a result we won't be able to give enough of it to the earth which depends on it. So we'll do it like this: we'll choose specific plants which we will grow and harvest in such a way that the resulting food will be very tightly compressed, pressed together so much that it becomes hard as a stone, and from this we'll be able to extract a large amount of formic acid.' These agricultural ants do this in order to produce as much formic acid as they possibly can. And these particular ants are ones that manage to put a lot of formic acid back into the soil. This is the connection I wanted you to see.

So you will also understand that poisons, even though they create inflammations or similar conditions, also function as chemicals with continuous healing effects, which counteract processes of dying. The bee in particular, you could say, is extremely important in this regard. The bee helps maintain the flowers' existence, and keeps them from dying out. This is why there is such a deep relationship between bees and flowers.

This stimulation of life becomes evident wherever insects

move about and are active on the earth. Wherever this happens, I would like to say, the earth has its store of poisons replenished—which means, of course, that death has been fended off and life has been preserved...

In the areas where we live, less attention is paid to such facts. But as you go further south you can hear farmers or peasants say, out of their instinctive knowledge, 'You must not disturb these ant colonies, because they prevent mould from becoming too destructive.' And those really alert to these things will say something else too. If you go for a walk with them through the woods, where trees have been felled and new ones are starting to grow, these people use their noses—they are very smart with their noses—and will, when they come to a certain area, say: 'Things will grow very well here. The mouldy odour is less strong here, so there must be an ant colony doing its job nearby.' There are people who can smell this. Based on a finely attuned sense of smell, many a farmer's saying has proven very useful...

22. The Harmony of Bees

Extract from a lecture given in Dornach on
26 November 1923

'Wherever we intrude upon . . . powers of nature, we tend to make things worse rather than better.' Here, as we move towards the area of human beings' handling and mishandling of the natural world, we come to the delicate harmony at work in bee colonies— also as an exemplary metaphor perhaps of a perfectly balanced give-and-take with nature which we can aspire to.

In nature there are remarkable connections between all things. The particular laws that people can't comprehend with their ordinary understanding are actually the most important. It is true, isn't it, that these laws operate in such a way as to allow always for a slight amount of freedom or latitude. For instance, take the balance between the sexes on earth. There is not a completely equal number of men and women in the world, but the number is approximately equal. Over the entire earth the number is just about equal, and this is controlled by nature's wisdom. If the time should ever come . . . when we are able to directly manipulate gender and leave the choice to parents, then things could become chaotic very quickly. Currently, when such things as wars decimate the population in a particular region, more children start being born there. In nature every deficiency or shortage calls forth an opposing response.

It is also true that when bees seek out nectar in a certain region they withdraw it from the plants . . . but the strange thing is that fruit trees and similar plants thrive better in regions where there is beekeeping than in regions where there isn't. When bees remove nectar from plants, nature does not stand idly by but creates still greater abundance. Thus we derive benefit not only from the honey which bees provide but also from enhanced fertility in plants which the bees have visited. This is an important law from which you can gain deep insights.

If you could see to the very depths of things you might say that nature has informed with a truly wonderful wisdom the entire way in which a bee colony functions. Bees respond to certain, extremely significant and wonderful powers of nature. That is why you will feel a certain reserve that should keep you from indiscriminately, and perhaps crudely, trying to pinpoint and manipulate these powers. It is still true today that whenever we intrude upon these powers of nature we tend to make things worse rather than better. But we don't worsen things immediately since nature everywhere puts boundaries or constraints in place, operating in the best way it can. We can remove certain constraints and seemingly make things a little easier for nature. For instance, it appears that we have aided nature a great deal by using the newer type of beehive boxes instead of the old-fashioned skeps—thus arranging things with both bee and human ease in mind.

But now we come to this whole new area of artificial breeding of bees. Gentlemen,[31] don't think I'm saying there isn't ... a great deal in favour of artificially breeding bees, because it does simplify quite a few things. But the strong bonding of a bee generation or species will be detrimentally affected over the longer term ... We'll have to wait and see how things look after 50 to 80 years. Certain forces that have regulated themselves in the beehive until now will become mechanized, will be carried out in a more artificial way. It won't be possible to establish the intimate relationship between a queen bee you have purchased and the worker bee in the way it would arise by itself in nature. But the effects of this are not apparent to begin with . . .

It does not hurt to be aware of the fact that by introducing a mechanical or artificial element we are actually disturbing what nature has produced in such a wonderful, self-regulating manner . . .

Extract from a lecture given in Dornach on 10 December 1923

The following three passages highlight bees' sensitivity to their surroundings: their intimate connection with their immediate, including human environment; and the importance of an equally sensitive human response to their needs.

American clover, with its perpetual blossoming, will eventually be abandoned because it doesn't improve the bees' blood. It stimulates the bees for a short time, just as you might stimulate someone with alcohol. The bees get all worked up and are able to work harder for a time. But one thing you should watch very carefully is not to introduce something completely foreign to the bees, since, by their very nature, they have become accustomed to and are connected with a specific area or region. You can see this by noting the variations in bees that come from different regions.

There is the central European bee, the common bee already mentioned. The Italian bee has a very different appearance; then the Carniolan bee is very different again from the Italian bee. Bees are very strongly attached to the region they belong to, and therefore you won't be able to impart any long-term benefit by giving them nectar derived from regions foreign to them. If you do this they will have to expend extra energy in converting the nectar within their bodies, and will experience turmoil as they try to convert it into a form similar to that which it takes in the place the clover comes from. You might be successful for a few years, but there will be real trouble later on...

Extract from a lecture given in Dornach on
1 December 1923

Consider also that a beekeeper doesn't approach a beehive in the same way any other person does. If I may say so, the bees feel a person's emanations, exhalations, vapours or perspiration. They know what makes up a specific human being, and become accustomed to this individual. If this person dies they have to break the relationship with one and gradually become accustomed to another. This is of great significance for bees...

You can find people who have green fingers when it comes to growing plants... Another puts in the same amount of effort, but nothing happens. It's due to a person's emanation, which influences flowers favourably in one case and unfavourably in another... So you can say that human beings can affect flowers—but they can affect bees even more strongly...

Extract from a lecture given in Dornach on
5 December 1923

Faced with the current decimation of bee populations and the rampant spread of disease in colonies all over the world, this passage, in which Steiner predicts the long-term harmful effects of artificial feeding and breeding methods, seems prophetic. Do we really know what we are doing when we meddle with nature, and introduce seemingly very practical and economically beneficial measures? One might think here also of GM crops. Perhaps, in that domain too, 80 or 100 years will have to pass before we reap the deleterious effects of what we have unleashed.

'Mr Müller cannot understand that bee colonies may die out in 80 or 100 years. He simply can't understand how Dr Steiner can say that, in 50 or 100 years, artificial breeding could cause serious problems for bee colonies...

In regard to the second point, about telling bees when the beekeeper dies, he has heard of a case where the majority of the hives died when the beekeeper tending them died. Just how this can happen he cannot understand...'

Let's investigate so that we can discuss this matter rationally: how can bees recognize the beekeeper who tends them... Imagine that you have a friend with whom you became acquainted in, say, 1915. This friend remains here in Europe, and you go to America and return again in 1925. [When you return] you see him and recognize him, remembering who he is. But what has happened meanwhile?... All the material substances in the human body are completely renewed or replaced over a period of seven or eight years. The old substances, such as cells, are completely exchanged for new ones. Nothing remains of what was there before ... but you recognize him nevertheless... He appears familiar, but if you were to examine him under a sufficiently large magnifying glass then you would see that ... blood magnified to a certain point no longer looks like blood but rather like many tiny dots resembling tiny creatures. These tiny dots are continually quivering and trembling. When you look at this you will see a great similarity between it and a horde of bees swarming about.

A person appears like a swarm of bees when you magnify sufficiently the substances contained in his body. Once you know this it might seem incomprehensible that one person could recognize another after ten years, because not a single one of these tiny creatures is still there. His eyes now have completely new 'dots'. There are new, different little creatures composing him, yet we still recognize each other after a long separation ... we recognize the whole person. Likewise the beehive isn't simply what you would call a collection of an indeterminate number of bees, but rather a complete whole, a whole being...

Our object of concern has nothing to do with the individual bees but rather with what belongs together to create the whole...

The change brought about by the death of the beekeeper does affect the whole hive in a certain way, this can't be denied...

You will get on well with bees only if you go beyond a normal, basic view of them and actually begin to pursue matters with an inner eye. The picture of things you get in this way is wonderful indeed. With this kind of insight you will have to say that a beehive is a total entity. You must try to understand it in its totality. And with such an entity, potential damage is not at all noticeable right away . . .

One 65-year-old person may be healthier than another, because the second one suffers from hardening of the arteries, or something similar. To observe this fact and link it with what happened to each in childhood is extremely interesting. For example, you can give a child milk that comes from cows that derive too much of their nourishment from plants growing in a soil with a high lime content. Through the cow's milk he drinks, the child absorbs some of the calcium present in the calcareous soil. Such excess calcium will not manifest itself immediately . . . But it turns out eventually that the child raised on mother's milk is still fresh in appearance at 65 or 66, while the other, raised on cow's milk, suffers hardening of the arteries at the same age.

Such things occur because a human being is a complete entity, and whatever happens at a given time may have much later after-effects . . . What I am trying to say is that it is very difficult, based on the current situation using artificial methods for feeding and breeding bees, to predict what significance such procedures will have in the future, 50, 60 or even 100 years from now . . .

It is one matter if you let nature take its course and only help to steer it in the right direction when necessary, but it is entirely another matter if you use artificial methods to speed things along . . . let's talk to each other again in a hundred

years, Mr Müller; then we'll see what kind of views you have
at that point . . .

Extract from a lecture given in Dornach on 3 February 1923

*The beehive is here seen as a kind of chaste vessel in which, through
the selfless, harmonious activity of its colony, a marvellous substance—honey—can be distilled from the whole environment.
Steiner spoke at length about bees, from many different perspectives, but this passage is a summation of his warm reverence for
these creatures, in response to what he saw as the love-made matter
arising from their tireless industry. Many people may not be fully
aware of the importance of bees for the continuation of a great
number of our crops. Perfectly attuned to their environment, they
keep biosystems in vibrant communication with one another and
constantly stimulate life and fertility. That they are now so stricken
by disease is one among many alarm bells that should spur us to a
more sensitive and less exploitative relationship with the natural
world.*

The question put by one of you gentlemen, who is an expert
on bees, pointed to the difference between the lives of bees
and of wasps. There is much that is similar . . . The life of the
beehive, however, is a remarkably strange one. What is its
basis? . . .

Much more so than among ants and wasps, life in the
beehive is based on the bees cooperating with each other
and accomplishing their tasks harmoniously. To under-

stand what causes this we must conclude that bees have a life in which the element that expresses itself in other animals in their sexual life is suppressed to an extraordinary degree...

You see, reproduction is taken care of in bees by a few select females, the queen bees. The sexual life of the others is really more or less suppressed. In sexual life, however, love is also inherent, as a soul element. Only because certain organs of the body are affected by this soul element do they manifest and express this love life. Inasmuch as this love is suppressed in bees, and concentrated only in one queen bee, what would otherwise be the bee's sexual life in the beehive is transferred to the other activities that the bees develop. This is why wise people of old, who saw things differently than we do today, associated this whole wondrous bustle of the beehive with the amorousness that is connected with the planet Venus.

So we can say that the wasps or ants are creatures that withhold themselves from the influence of the planet Venus, whereas the bees are completely given up to its influence, and develop a love life that permeates the entire hive... The soul element that arises in us only when our hearts love is tangibly present throughout the hive. Most of the individual bees renounce love, but therefore develop love throughout the hive as a whole. We can begin to understand their life if we realize that bees live as though in an atmosphere that is wholly pervaded by love.

It is most beneficial to the bee that it sustains itself from the parts of the plant that are wholly permeated with the love life of the plant. The bee sucks its nourishment, which it then turns into honey, from those parts of the plant that are integral to its love life. The bee thus bears the love life of the flowers back into the hive. This is why we must study the life of the bee from a soul perspective...

The bee is really alone in ... renouncing an individual sex life and instead becoming a bearer of love. Bees indeed carry into the hive what lives in flowers. If you really begin to think this through you can uncover the whole mystery of the bee-hive. The life of this sprouting, thriving love that is spread over the flowers is then also contained in the honey...

Nothing is better for human beings than to add the right amount of honey to their food. In a marvellous way the bee really sees to it that we learn to use our soul to work upon our bodily organs. By means of honey the beehive gives us what we need to ensure our soul works industriously on our body. When we add honey to our meal we prepare the soul to work and breathe properly in the body. Beekeeping is therefore something that contributes very significantly to civilization, because it strengthens us... When we look at a beehive we should say to ourselves, with something akin to exaltation, that the whole universe enters us through the beehive, and makes us more capable human beings...

Part Six:

ANIMAL BEINGS

23. Bird, Lion, Cow

Extract from a lecture given in Dornach on 19 October 1923

Moving now to the world of mammals and birds, we begin with a passage that seeks to enter imaginatively and sensitively into the archetypal qualities of three animal types, and relate them to different aspects of the human being. Scientists may object that relating animals to the human being does not allow full scope for their own inherent qualities. Yet Steiner's descriptions are, it seems to me, as alive and close to the reality of these creatures as perhaps a Native American's intimate reverence for the eagle or buffalo; and this connection between human being and animal is one we urgently need to rekindle in an ecological age. By relating the eagle to the head and senses, the lion to the heart and breathing, and the cow to digestion, Steiner is not giving us dry stereotypes, but an enlivening sense both of our own nature and the whole natural world.

The lion can really only be understood if we develop a feeling for the joy, the inner satisfaction that lions have in living together with their whole environment. There is really no other animal, except for those related to the lion, which has such a wonderful, mysterious breathing process. In all animal nature the breathing rhythms must harmonize with the rhythms of blood circulation. The two rhythms differ in that the rhythms of the circulation grow heavy because of the digestive system that is tied up with them, and the breathing rhythms grow light in the attempt to achieve the near-weightless state of the physical brain. In birds, anything that lives in their breathing really lives at the same time in the head. A bird is all head and in a way outwardly represents the head in the world. Its thoughts are in its plumage. For anyone with a real feeling for the beauty of nature there is hardly anything more moving than to experience the inner connection between human thought—when it is really engaged, inwardly teeming with life—and the plumage of a bird. Anyone who is inwardly practised in such things knows exactly when he is thinking like a peacock, an eagle or a sparrow. Apart from the fact that one is astral and the other physical, these things do actually correspond in a wonderful way ... And it may be said that the breathing predominates to such an extent in a bird's life that other processes—the circulation and so on—are almost negligible. All the heaviness of digestion that imposes itself on the circulation is completely removed, lifted away by the bird's sense of itself.

In the lion a kind of balance exists between breathing and circulation. The lion's circulation is certainly also weighed down, but not as much as a camel's, for instance, or a cow's. In them the digestion burdens the circulation to a tremendous degree. In the lion, whose digestive tract is comparatively short and constituted in such a way that the digestive process is accomplished as rapidly as possible, digestion does not burden the circulation to any marked degree. On the other hand, the head principle has developed in such a way in the lion's head that breathing is held in balance with the rhythm of circulation. In lions, more than any other animal, the inner rhythms of breathing and heartbeat are in inner balance and harmony. This is why lions—if we enter into what may be called their subjective life—have that particular way of devouring their food with unbridled voracity, literally gulping it down. They are simply glad to have got it down. They are ravenous for nourishment because it is part of their nature that hunger causes them much more pain than it does other animals. They are greedy for nourishment but they are not bent on being fastidious gourmets! They are not at all interested in taste sensations for they are animals that find their inner satisfaction in the even rhythms of their breathing and circulation. It is only when the food has passed over into the blood which regulates the heartbeat, and when the heartbeat has come into reciprocal action with the breathing—it is a source of enjoyment to lions to draw breath and gives them deep inner satisfaction—it is only when they feel in themselves the result of their feeding, an inner balance between breathing and circulation, that lions are really in their element. They are wholly lion when they experience the deep inner satisfaction of the blood beating upwards and the breath pulsing downwards. Lions are most fully alive and in their element when these two wave movements interpenetrate.

Look at a lion, how it runs, how it leaps, how the head is held, even the look in its eye; and you will see that all this arises from a continuous rhythmical interplay between losing inner balance and restoring balance again. Hardly anything else strikes us as more mysterious than the remarkable look in a lion's eye; so much is revealed there of inward mastery, the mastering of opposing forces. That is what we perceive in the look in a lion's eye: the heartbeat controlled by the breathing rhythm.

And again, let those who have an artistic eye for form look at the shape of the lion's mouth; this shows how the heartbeat pulses upwards as far as the mouth, but is held back by the breath. If you could really picture the way the heartbeat and breathing interrelate, you would arrive at the shape of the lion's mouth.

The lion is all chest. In this animal the rhythmical system comes to perfect expression both in the outer form and in the way of life. Lions are organized in such a way that the interplay between heartbeat and breathing also comes to expression in the reciprocal relationship of heart and lungs.

We really have to say, therefore, that if we look for what most closely resembles the bird in the human being, in metamorphosed form of course, we come to the human head; if we look for what most closely resembles the lion, it is the region of the human chest, where the rhythms of circulation and breathing meet.

Let us now turn our attention away from everything we perceive as the bird kingdom up there in the air, and from everything that lives in rhythmic circulation of the air in the earth's immediate environment, for example in the lion. Let us consider the ox or cow. I have often spoken of the pleasure to be gained from watching a herd of cattle lying replete and satisfied in a meadow, and from observing the process of digestion which here again manifests in the position of the body, the expression of the eyes, in every movement. Take the opportunity to observe a cow lying in the meadow and its reaction when a noise comes from one direction or another. It is really marvellous to see how the animal raises its head; how in this lifting there lies the feeling that it is all heaviness, that it is not easy for a cow to lift its head; there is something rather special going on. Seeing a cow in a meadow disturbed in this way it seems clear that the cow is amazed at having to raise its head for anything other than grazing... Just look at the way the cow does this. This is what goes on when a cow lifts its head. But it is not limited to the movement of the head. You cannot imagine a lion lifting its head the way a cow does. This lies in the shape of the head. And if we further observe the animal's whole form we see that it is in fact what I may call a complete and wholesale digestion system! The weight of the digestion burdens the circulation to such a degree that it overwhelms everything to do with the head and breathing. The animal is all digestion. It is truly marvellous, if one looks with the eye of the spirit, to turn one's gaze upwards to the birds and then downwards to the cow...

If we now want to look for similar things in the human being, for something corresponding to what in the cow is a one-sided development, the physical embodiment of a certain astral element, we find it in the human digestive organs and their continuation in the limbs—harmoniously interwoven with what else is there. The things I see in the eagle high in the air above me, and in the animal that rejoices in the atmosphere around him as a lion does, and in the animal connected with earth forces that arise from below and are also active in the digestive organs ... I find all three configurations united into one, harmonized and balanced in the human being. I find the metamorphosis of the bird in the human head, the metamorphosis of the lion in the human chest and the metamorphosis of the cow in the digestive system and the limbs—but again, utterly metamorphosed and transformed.

If we contemplate such things today and realize again that the human being is actually born out of the whole of nature, that he bears the whole of nature within him as I have shown, that he bears the bird kingdom, the lion kingdom and the essential nature of the cow in him, then we have specific aspects of what is expressed in the more abstract phrase: the human being is a microcosm. He is indeed a microcosm, and the macrocosm is within him; and all the creatures that live in the air, all the animals on the face of the earth whose special element is the air that circulates there, and the animals whose special element is below the surface of the earth in the forces of gravity—all these work together in us as a harmonious whole, so that we are a synthesis of eagle, lion and ox or cow...

The human chest—the heartbeat and breathing—must, if it desires to grasp itself as one of the secrets of nature, turn its gaze to such a thing as the nature of the lion. And the human being must try to understand his metabolic system from the constitution and organization of the cow or ox. But in our head we have the vehicle of our thoughts, in the chest the vehicle for feeling and in the metabolic system the vehicle for the will. So in his soul nature too the human being is an image of the thoughts that move through the world with the birds and find expression in their plumage; and of the world of feeling that encompasses the earth, found in the lion in the balanced life of heartbeat and breathing. This is toned down in us, but still represents the quality of inner courage... And if we wish to find the will impulses predominantly connected with metabolism, to embody them in outer form as it were, we need to look to what has assumed physical form in the cow...

Mahatma Gandhi ... is a man who certainly directs his attention entirely to outer affairs but at the same time represents something like an eighteenth-century rationalist among Indian people and in relation to the Hindu religion. Remarkably he has, nevertheless, retained veneration of the cow in his enlightened Hinduism. This cannot be set aside, says Mahatma Gandhi who, as you know, was sentenced to six years' imprisonment by the British for his political activities in India. He still retains veneration of the cow.

Things such as these, which have so tenaciously persisted

in more spiritual cultures, can only be understood when one is aware of the inner connections, when one really knows the tremendous secrets that lie in the ruminating animal, in the cow. Then we can understand why people come to venerate in the cow a sublime astrality that has, as it were, become earthly, and only in this respect more lowly...

24. Cow and Stag

Extract from a lecture given in Koberwitz, Silesia, on
12 June 1924

*Here again we encounter a perception of subtle gestures in the
animal kingdom; of apparently slight yet profound differences
between two animals. Learning to perceive, for instance, the quivering sensitivity of a deer or the more self-contained sufficiency of
a cow, and allowing these differences to resonate in us, is a step
towards deep attunement with the natural world.*

Have you ever thought why cows have horns but certain other
animals have antlers? That's an extremely important question. However, what science has to offer on this point is
usually very one-sided and superficial. Let us try to answer
the question of why cows have horns. Remember that I said a
living creature need not just have forces that radiate outwards, but can also have forces that stream inwards . . . A cow
has horns and also hooves. What happens at these places
where horns and hooves grow? At these places the streams of
energy are turned back inwards especially strongly, and the
outside world is shut off particularly strongly. All interaction
with the external world, such as occurs through skin or hair,
is curtailed. In this way the development of horns and hooves
is connected to the form and development of the animal as a
whole.

Antler formation is something wholly different. In the case
of antlers, the streams are not directed back into the organism; instead they serve as outlets so that certain streams can

be directed outwards and discharged into the external world. ('Streams' don't always have to be fluid or gaseous but can also be streams of energy, which in this case are focused in the antlers.) A stag is beautiful because it stands in intense communication with its surroundings, because it directs outwards some of its energy streams, and lives in quivering, sensitive unity with its environment. It thereby absorbs everything that influences nerves and senses at an organic level. A stag thus becomes a quick and nervous animal. In a certain respect, all animals with antlers are suffused with a slight nervousness, which can already be seen in their eyes.

A cow, on the other hand, has horns to send the formative astral and etheric forces[32] back into its digestive system . . .

25. The Beaver

Extract from a lecture given in Dornach on 10 January 1923

Study of nature has to be based on painstaking and precise observation. But that alone is not enough, and using words such as 'instinct' to explain animal behaviour is not really an explanation at all. Here Steiner seeks a deeper insight into the behaviour of the beaver, locating this in the power of its tail to absorb sunlight, and with it an intelligence that only comes fully into its own as autumn approaches. While Steiner offers no definite proof of these statements, we can take them at least as a further elaboration of the idea that intelligence is not something 'produced' by the brain but, rather, absorbed from the cosmos to the extent that the physical 'vessel' makes this possible. The social life of beavers can in some ways be seen to express and embody the universal cooperation of nature rather than the 'survival of the fittest' propounded by Darwin. While competition between species is of course a ubiquitous reality, a deeper or broader view can see such competitiveness as a wonderful means of self-regulation in the earth organism, comparable to the essential death—as well as growth—of cells in the human body.

What I will relate to you is especially connected with the beavers in Canada...

Such a beaver has rather a clumsy head and body, the front legs are quite thick and the hind feet webbed so he can swim. The strangest feature is the tail, which looks almost like a tool; it is quite flat and is, in fact, the beaver's most ingenious aspect. Behind him he carries his most ingenious tool...

The beaver is a most unusual animal. When one becomes acquainted with it in its own habitat, one discovers it is an extremely phlegmatic animal, as is also evident in our zoos. It is so phlegmatic that . . . you can attack it, or grab at it, and it will not defend itself. The beaver will never attack, however much it is provoked; it is an entirely phlegmatic creature.

These beavers live mainly in areas such as large swamps or small rivers, and they live in a most remarkable way. When spring arrives a beaver looks for a spot near a lake or river, digs a burrow in the mud and spends the entire summer living like a recluse alone in this burrow. This beaver sits the whole summer in its reclusive dwelling like a phlegmatic monk . . .

When winter approaches—already when late autumn comes—the beavers emerge from their burrows and congregate in groups of two to three hundred. They come in all their 'phlegma' and form communities. Naturally, those that had mated previously are among them. A female beaver will have prepared her isolated home so that it is ready for offspring, while the male has been living nearby in his own burrow. Now, all these families gather together.

In their slow, phlegmatic way, the beavers proceed to look for a suitable locality. Though it is sometimes hard to observe because of their sluggish temperament, one group will prefer a lake, and another a river, which they follow downstream to a point that seems particularly suited to their purposes. After they have investigated the area the whole group gathers again. Near the lake or river there are usually trees. And now it is remarkable how these clumsy beavers suddenly become extraordinarily skilful. They use their front feet—not their hind feet which are webbed so they can swim—more cleverly than a person handles his tools. Using their front paws and sharp teeth they gnaw branches off trees, and even cut through tree trunks. Then, when a group of them has enough branches and felled trees, they drag them either into the lake they have chosen or into the river.

These animals then push the branches and trees in the lake to their selected spot. Those who have dragged their trees into the river know full well that the river itself will carry them. They only steer the branches so that they won't drift to the side. In this way all the branches and trees are transported to the spot they have chosen either on the lake's shore or beside the stream.

Having arrived there, those who have chosen a lake—having transported the trees to the shore—immediately begin constructing so-called lodges. The others, which have chosen a river, do not start with the building of lodges but first construct a network of interlaced branches [*see sketch*]. When the beavers have built a wall like this they add a second by fetching more branches, all of the same length. In this way they make a wall two metres or more thick. In this way they dam up the river; the water has to flow over it, and underneath they have a free space. Only now, having finished their dam, do they build their lodge into this wall so that the river flows over it.

Once the beavers have accumulated enough branches, and their wall appears thick enough to them, they haul in other

material such as ordinary lumps of earth. They fashion a kind of loam from it, and putty up the dam on all sides. The beavers first erect a wall, just like real architects. Those who choose a lake site, however, don't need a dam and therefore don't try to build one.

After this wall is built—in the case of the beavers on the lake this begins immediately—they start to construct little lodges from the same material. These look like clay barrels [*see sketch*], but they are real little houses, constructed like braided mats. They are puttied up so well that the small amount of water that seeps into the space can do the beavers no harm. A beaver lodge of this kind is never built in a part of the stream where the water freezes. Just think how ingenious this is! As you know, water only freezes on its surface; if you dive deep enough you come to still or flowing water, neither of which freeze at that depth. At exactly the level where the water never freezes, these beavers build their dwellings.

Each of these lodges has two floors. There is a floor built in here [*sketching*] and below is the entrance. The beavers can

run up and down in the lodge; they live upstairs and keep their winter supplies downstairs. They haul in the food they need for the winter, and when it is all stored the beaver family moves into this lodge, always remaining near to the other families.

Here the beaver families live until spring, when they once again move to their solitary dwellings. During the winter, food supplies are brought up from the lower floor, and thus the beavers sustain themselves. As I said, when summer comes they seek out their solitary burrows, but during the winter they are together, leading a social life in beaver villages on the bottom of lakes or in streams by the side of the dam which they have built so skilfully.

From all that has been observed, even beavers in zoos work solely with their teeth and front paws, never with their tails. Although it is so ingeniously formed, the tail is never used for work...

One can say that the beaver as a single individual appears to be very sluggish ... yet together with others it accomplishes all these extraordinarily clever feats. We can say therefore that Rosegger's saying about human beings does not apply to beavers: 'One's human, two are a crowd, and three a bunch of animals.'... We can say the opposite is true of beavers. One is dull-witted but several are a bit brighter! When two or three hundred gather together in the autumn, they become very clever indeed, real architects...

Now much research could be done on why the beavers are so clever when they congregate. An important indication is the fact that they begin their activity in the autumn; by day, however, one sees little of this activity. The construction of such a dam and beaver village—it's really a whole village— takes place very quickly and is often finished in a matter of days. They are seen doing little during the day, extraordinarily little, but they work feverishly at night. Thus the beaver's cleverness is brought about first by winter and second by night. This provides the real clues for studying the whole thing...

Where does the beaver spend the summer? It stays in the ground in its solitary burrow, allowing heat and light that enter the burrow to permeate its body, so that it actually absorbs all the summer sunlight and warmth. When this absorption is complete in the autumn, the beaver begins to look for other beavers, and together they become clever. It employs a cleverness that it does not possess as a single individual...

This clearly illustrates what I said last time:[33] the intelligence in a creature must first be gathered, just as water is collected in a bucket. While the beaver lives as a single animal in its summer house it gathers and accumulates sunlight and the sun's warmth—or so we say, because all we can perceive of the sun is its light and warmth. In truth, the beaver gathers its intelligence. Along with sunlight and warmth, intelligence streams from the cosmos down upon the earth, and the beaver gathers it for itself; and then the beaver has it and it builds...

Something else now becomes comprehensible: the beaver's tail. Compare it with what I said about the dog's tail, which is the latter's organ of pleasure and therefore the organ of its soul expression. The dog wags its tail when it is happy. In the beaver's case the tail, which the animal does not use as a tool but which is formed most ingeniously, contains its accumulated intelligence. The animal directs itself by means of this.[34] In other words, the beaver is really directed by the sun's warmth and light. These are contained in the tail and have become intelligence. This warmth and light are really the communal intelligence of the beaver colony.

These tails are the means by which the sunlight and warmth produce cleverness. The beaver does not employ its tail as a physical instrument, but uses its front paws and teeth for this purpose. The tail, however, is something that has an effect—just as when a group is being driven forward by somebody from behind. In that case someone is driving them forward, but here it is the sun's power which, through the beaver's tails, still has an after-effect in winter and constructs the beaver village. It is this intelligence, descending from the sun to the earth with light and warmth, that does the building through them . . .

Anybody can call animal behaviour 'instinct', which is just a word. Such words are like empty containers into which everything is poured that one knows nothing about. If one wishes to explain something like instinct, however, one reaches the point where one has to say that the sun is at work here . . . and one comes to recognize how the earth's cosmic surroundings affect living creatures . . .

The beavers use this intelligence as groups, not individuals. Individually they could never accomplish what they do . . . whereas human beings have their individual soul.

I once told you what the human thighbone looks like, for example. In the beaver it really isn't the same, but a human thighbone looks like an extraordinarily delicate, beautiful work of art. In it there are ingeniously constructed arches. A human being is actually constructed in such a way that, when observing him correctly, one can say that he builds up everything in himself that the beaver constructs outwardly . . . The question then arises: where does all that is so wisely and ingeniously constructed within a human being originate? If

the beaver construction originates from the sun and its surroundings, the human being's organization also derives from
the sun... If facts are viewed correctly they lead you to
realize that the world is really a unity and that we are also
dependent upon ... not merely a shining, warming sun, but
also a sun of intelligence ...

26. One with the Animals

The following two passages, which end Part Six, reiterate, as a prelude to Part Seven's concern with agriculture, the profound nature of the animal kingdom and the importance of our reverent, non-exploitative relationship with it. There is a great qualitative difference between the kind of view expressed here and the Darwinian perspective. While this latter view does see us as evolving from—and therefore in a certain way thanks to—the animal kingdom, the idea of natural selection introduces a sense of combat and conquest into our relationship with nature, whereas Steiner's words conjure a mood of underlying interdependence, gratitude and love.

Extract from a lecture given in Hamburg on 17 May 1910

What is more natural than to ask how animal life and animal fate are related to what we call the course of human karma?[35] In this we shall find included what are, to mankind, the most important and profound questions of destiny.

The relation of human beings on the earth to the animal kingdom differs with the various epochs and also between various peoples. It is certainly not without interest to see that in the case of cultures which have preserved the best parts of humanity's ancient, sacred wisdom there is a deeply sympathetic and loving treatment of animals. For example, in the Buddhist world, which has preserved important conceptions of the world held by mankind in ancient times, we find a very sympathetic treatment of animals, a treatment and a feeling towards the animal kingdom which many people in Europe cannot understand.

You will find it among other peoples too, especially where a nation has preserved some of the old conceptions... An instance is the Arab and his treatment of his horse. On the other hand one may say that in those countries in which a contemporary view of the world prevails—that is, in the West—there is little understanding of such sympathy with the animal kingdom. It is characteristic too that in the Middle Ages and on into our own times, precisely in those countries where Christianity has spread, the idea has arisen that animals cannot be considered as beings with their own particular soul life, but rather as something like automata...

It is the fate of the peoples of the West—if we may say so—that they have to work up from materialistic foundations, and in the conquering of these materialistic views and tendencies they will develop the forces that will lead to the highest spiritual life. It is a consequence of this destiny, this karma, that the peoples of the West have a tendency to consider animals only as exploitable automata. Whoever cannot penetrate into the working of spiritual life and can only judge by what surrounds him in the external sense world would, from the impressions of that world, easily arrive at an idea about the animal kingdom which simply places the animals at a lower level. On the other hand, conceptions of the world that contain elements of primordial spiritual truths, the ancient wisdom of humanity, preserved a kind of knowledge of what exists spiritually in the animal kingdom; and in spite of all this misunderstanding, in spite of all that has crept into their views of the world and destroyed their purity, they have not been able to forget that spiritual activities and spiritual laws are active in the life and development of the animal kingdom...

We have only evolved as humanity by freeing ourselves

from the creatures which live around us in the lower king-doms of nature. At one time we were bound up with these creatures, with all their forces, in the stress of evolution—like the denser constituents in a fluid solution. We have uplifted ourselves from them and in this way our evolution has been made possible. Thus we look upon the three kingdoms of nature around us, and see in them something which had to form a basis for our development. These beings have sunk in order that we might be able to rise. In this manner we look upon the subordinate kingdoms of nature from the proper aspect . . .

We can look upon the animals and say: 'All that animals manifest in the way of cruelty, voracity, and all animal vices, and also the skill and innate wisdom they have, we also would have had if we had not been able to rise above them. We *owe* this liberation of our astral bodies to the circumstance that all the grosser astral bodies have remained behind in the animal kingdom and the earth.'

Thus the animals have the astral body in common with us, and are therefore able to feel pain. But from what has now been said we see that they do not possess the power to evolve through pain and through the conquest of pain, for they have no individual ego. The animals are on this account much more to be pitied than us. We have to bear pain, but each pain is for us a means to perfection; through overcoming it we rise higher. We have left behind us the animal as some-thing that already has the capacity to feel pain but does not yet possess the power to raise itself above pain, and to triumph by means of it. That is the fate of the animals. They manifest to us our own former organization, when we were capable of feeling pain but could not yet, through over-coming the pain, transform it into something beneficial for humanity. Thus in the course of our earthly evolution we have left our worst aspects to the animals, and they stand around us as tokens of how we ourselves came to our relative perfection. We should not have got rid of the dregs of our own nature had we not left the animals behind. We must learn to consider such facts, not as theories, but rather with a sense of universality...

We can then experience a great and all-embracing feeling of sympathy for the animal kingdom. Hence, when this universal feeling sprang from the primeval wisdom of humanity, when mankind still possessed the remembrance of the original knowledge which told each person, through a dim clairvoyant vision, how things once were, this was accompanied by a high degree of sympathy for the animal kingdom. This sympathy will return when people accustom themselves to the insights of spiritual science, and when they again see how the karma of humanity is bound up with the whole world's karma.

Extract from a lecture given in Cologne on 7 June 1908

When human beings develop a strong, feeling connection with animals, this actively attracts real forces and beings. Those who find this hard to contemplate might see it at least as an imaginative description of a powerful life-engendering resonance between different realms.

It is especially where the different kingdoms of nature come into contact with each other that various different kinds of elemental beings reveal themselves: within the bowels of the earth, where rock and veins of metal ore meet; at a spring, where moss spreads upon stone, so that plant and mineral kingdoms come into contact; or where plant and animal meet, for example where a bee enters a flower; and also where the human being and the animal encounter one another. But in the latter case such beings do not appear in the mundane encounters of everyday life, for instance when a butcher slaughters an ox or someone eats meat. They appear, rather, when two realms meet in an excess and outpouring of life forces. In particular they arise where someone has the kind of relationship with animals that particularly engages his thoughts and feelings. A shepherd, for example, may have this kind of special connection with his sheep. Such feeling connections were very common in former times, resembling the relationship which an Arab has to his horse, rather than that of a racing-stable owner. When soul forces play over from one realm into another—as they do between a shepherd and his lambs, or when effusions of smell and taste stream from the flowers towards the bees—certain beings find an opportunity to incarnate.

Part Seven:

CULTURE AND AGRICULTURE

27. Education for Ecology

Extract from a lecture given in Torquay on 14 August 1924

If children are given a sense for the living earth and their connection with it when young, they will develop into adults who on the one hand are more securely rooted in themselves, and on the other are more capable of acting as caring custodians of the natural world.

If you put single plants in front of the child and use them to demonstrate different things, you are doing something that has no reality. A plant by itself is not a reality. If you pull out a hair and examine it as though it were a thing by itself, that would not be a reality either. In ordinary life we say everything is real whose outlines we can see with our eyes. But if you look at a stone and form some opinion about it, that is one thing; if you look at a hair or a rose, it is another. In ten years' time the stone will be exactly as it is now, but in two days the rose will have changed. The rose is only a reality together with the whole rose bush. The hair is nothing in itself but is only a reality when considered with the whole head, as part of the whole human being...

Here we have a plant [*draws*] but this alone is not the plant, for the soil beneath it also belongs to the plant, spread out on all sides and maybe for a very long way. There are some plants that send out little roots a very long way. And when you realize that the small clod of earth containing the plant belongs to a much greater area of soil around it, then you will see how necessary it is to manure the earth to promote healthy plant growth...

Under no circumstances can you understand any plant properly if you examine it by itself. If you go (on foot preferably) to a district where there are certain geological formations such as red sandstone, and look at the plants there, you will find that most of them have reddish-yellow flowers. The flowers belong to the soil. Soil and plant form a unity, just as your head and hair also form a whole.

So you shouldn't teach geography and geology by themselves, and then botany separately. That is absurd. Geography must be taught together with a description of the country and observation of the plants, for the earth is an organism and the plants are like the hair of this organism. Children must be able to see that the earth and the plants belong together, and that each kind of soil bears the plants that belong to it.

Thus the only right way to speak of plants is in connection with the earth, and to give children a clear feeling that the earth is a living being on which hair grows ...

Children can only understand how to cultivate the land if they know how the soil is really part of the plant ... In many districts over the last 50 or 60 years all agricultural produce has degenerated ... Why is this so? It is because people do not know how to make the soil alive by using manure. It is impossible for them to understand this if they have been taught that plants are distinct in themselves, in some way separate from the earth. The plant is no more an object in itself than a hair is. For if this were so you might expect it to grow just as well in a piece of wax or tallow as on the skin of the head. But it only grows on the skin ...

Children should feel from the very beginning that they are standing on a living earth. This is of great significance for their whole life ... Children rejoice inwardly if they hear about the plant world in connection with the earth.

Similarly, we should consider how to introduce our children to the animal world . . . Humans are not as majestic as the lion but they have something of majesty in them. They are not as cruel as the tiger but they have a certain cruelty. They are not as patient as sheep but they have some patience. They are not as lazy as the donkey—at least, not everybody!—but they have some of this laziness in them. All human beings . . . bear all these within them, but harmonized. All the qualities tone each other down, as it were, and the human being is . . . the synthesis of all the different soul qualities that the animal possesses. The goal of the human being is to have the right dose of lion-ness, sheep-ness, tiger-ness, donkey-ness and so on . . .

You can find that the human being's external form, also, has in a modified, harmonized form what is distributed among the animals. For instance, think of a waddling duck; you have a relic of this waddling part between your fingers, only shrunk . . . Imagine you were made of elastic that could be pulled out in varying degrees in different directions; stretching you in one direction would give one kind of animal; or if the upper part of your face, say, were pushed up and stretched . . . then another animal would arise. Thus humans bear the whole animal kingdom within them . . . You can teach about the animal kingdom by considering it as a human being spread out into all the different animal forms. This will give children a very beautiful, delicate feeling . . . They will grow together with all the kingdoms of the earth. They no longer merely stand on the dead ground of the earth but on the living ground, for they feel the earth as something living. They gradually come to think of themselves standing on the earth as though they were standing on some great, living creature, like a whale. This is the right feeling. This alone can lead them to a really human feeling about the world . . .

Why is it that people go about in the world today as though they had lost their roots? Anyone can see that people do not walk properly nowadays; they do not step properly but drag their legs after them. They learn differently in sports activities, but there too there is something unnatural about their movements. But above all they have no idea how to think or what to do with their lives. They know what to do well enough if you put them in front of a sewing machine or telephone, or if an excursion or a world tour is being arranged. But they do not know what to do out of themselves because their education has not led them to find their right place in the world. You cannot put this right by coining phrases about educating people properly, but only if you find the right way of speaking, specifically and in detail about the plants in their true relationship to the soil and of the animals in their rightful place beside humanity. Then human beings will stand on earth as they should and will have the right attitude towards the world . . .

28. The Farm as Living Organism

The passages below, all drawn from the 'Agriculture Course'
which Steiner gave to farmers in 1923, elaborate in great detail on
Steiner's vision for a revitalizing of agriculture. His 'biodynamic'
method was not only the forerunner of organic farming, but in
several respects goes beyond it in an effort to return to soil and crops
the full vitality they once had. Here again, before the full advent of
industrial farming methods, we can see how prescient Steiner was
in seeing approaching dangers and taking steps to remedy them.

Extract from a lecture given in Koberwitz, Silesia, on
10 June 1924

The truly self-sufficient and self-sustaining farm is a complete
organism in which everything is of reciprocal benefit to everything
else. In this overall organism every 'organ'—soil, crops, animals
and even the farmer himself—interacts harmoniously. This is light
years away from a materialistic agriculture, which adds chemicals
to get results but overlooks the weakening effect of this on bio-
diversity, animal and plant vitality, and nutritional value. In
Steiner's view as described here, the farmer is a kind of artist in
tune with his material—the land—and sensitive to its changing
needs.

Now a farm comes closest to its own essence when it can be
conceived as a kind of independent individuality, a self-
contained entity. In reality, every farm ought to aspire to this
state of being a self-contained individuality. This cannot be

entirely achieved, but we need to aspire towards it. This means that within our farms we should attempt to have everything we need for agricultural production, including of course the right numbers of livestock. From an ideal perspective, any manure and so forth introduced from outside the farm would have to be regarded as remedies for an ailing farm. A healthy farm would be one that can produce everything it needs from within itself. We shall see in a moment why this is so . . .

Let us begin today from the point of view that takes the soil as the foundation of agriculture . . .

We usually think of the soil . . . as being something purely mineral, with organic matter added to it only incidentally to the extent that humus develops or manure is applied. That the soil might contain not just this kind of life but also an inherent, plantlike vitality and even something of the nature of soul qualities is scarcely conceived of. And if we go even further and see how this inner life of the soil—in terms of its tiniest constituents I would like to say—is quite different in summer than in winter, we then enter domains that are of tremendous significance for practical life but which at present no one takes any account of. Indeed, if we take the soil as our point of departure we will have to recognize that it functions as a kind of organ within the overall organism revealed wherever nature shows growth.

The soil is a real organ, one which we can compare to the human diaphragm. We gain the right idea of what is present there if we imagine that organs in the human head are located above the diaphragm . . . while other organs are located below it. The comparison is not precise but is good enough for purposes of illustration. If we compare the soil to a human diaphragm we must then say that the head of the individuality of the farm is underground, and that we, and all our farm animals, are living as it were in its belly. Everything above ground actually belongs to the bowels of what we can call this agricultural individuality. When we walk round a farm we are in a way walking through its belly, and the crops are growing up into its belly. So this individuality is standing on its head.

Now why do I say that the 'agricultural individuality' is standing on its head? I say this because what is in the immediate vicinity of the earth—the air, atmosphere, water vapour and warmth in which we live and breathe, and from which the plants also obtain their external heat, air and water—in fact corresponds to the human being's abdominal organs. Conversely, everything below ground that affects plant growth is similar to the effect that our head has on our body—most notably during childhood but also to some extent throughout life. A lively exchange is continually taking place between what is above and below ground . . .

As far as plant growth is concerned, we must look underground for the effects of the heavens, and above ground for the effects of the earth's more immediate environment. Thus what comes from the heavens and affects plant growth works less through direct radiation than through being first absorbed by the ground and radiated upwards . . .

Everything going on in the 'belly', in the air above ground, constitutes a kind of digestion for the plants, and this digestion . . . must be drawn down into the ground so that a real interplay takes place. All the forces and fine homoeopathic dilutions produced by the water and air above ground are drawn down by the soil's greater or lesser lime content . . .

Whereas the cosmic factor is associated more with the earth's interior and works upwards into the upper parts of the plant, the earthly factor is localized above ground but works downwards, drawn into the plant with the help of substances such as lime. Look at plants in which lime strongly pulls the earth factor right down into the root. These are plants that send out branching roots in all directions, like good fodder plants, that is, plants such as sainfoin,[36] rather than crops like beet or turnips. Thus, if we want to learn to understand plants, we need to be able to tell from their form and the colour of their flowers to what extent cosmic and earthly factors are at work in them . . .

Suppose we want to hold in check everything that tries to stream upwards through the stem into the leaves; suppose we want to keep it down below in the plant's root system . . . We have to plant it in sandy soil because this holds the cosmic forces in check, really holds them fast. In the case of potatoes we want to keep back the flowering process below in the tubers—which are not true roots at all but rhizomes—as stems that have been held in check. To hold cosmic forces in check [that would otherwise strive towards flowering] we must plant our potatoes in sandy soil.

From all this we can see that the ABC of nurturing plant growth is to know what is cosmic and what is terrestrial or earthly in a plant. We need to know how to adjust the composition of the soil, for instance so that the cosmic factor can become more dense, held back as it were in roots and leaves; or conversely, how to make it finer so that it can more readily be sucked up into the flowers, giving them colour, or into the fruits, permeating them with fine flavour . . .

If we human beings, with what we know today, had to try to develop all the many modern varieties of fruit from the relatively few varieties of primeval times, we would not get very far. Fortunately for us, the forms of our different fruit varieties already became hereditary back in a time when humanity's intuitive, primeval wisdom still knew how to create them from primitive varieties...

What our friend Stegemann said about being able to notice a decline in the quality of agricultural produce was very much to the point... Natural gifts, naturally inherited knowledge, traditional medicines, and so on that have been passed down from ancient times are all losing their vigour. We need to acquire new knowledge to be able to enter into all these interrelationships again. Humanity has only two choices: either to start once again, in every field of endeavour, to learn from the whole of nature, from relationships with the whole cosmos, or to allow both nature and human life to degenerate and die off. There is no other choice. Today, no less than in ancient times, we are in need of knowledge that can really enter fully into the inner workings of nature...

Now the plants growing on the earth are not the only thing to consider—a certain complement of animal life also belongs to each region of the earth. For reasons that will become apparent ... we cannot disregard the animals because the best infusion of cosmic qualities, if I can put it like that, takes place in the interaction between the plants and animals of a given area. The strange thing is that if a farm has the right number of cows, horses and other animals, the manure provided by these animals adds up to just the amount needed by the farm... This is due to the fact that the animals will consume the right amount of plants which the land provides and, through their metabolic processes, will produce just the right amount of manure needed to return to the land...

The cosmic influences that come to expression in a plant come from the interior of the earth, as I said, and are led upwards. Thus, if a plant especially rich in these cosmic influences is eaten by an animal, the manure that the animal's digestive system provides as a result of consuming such fodder will be just the right thing for the soil where that plant grows ...

Manure

Animal dung is plant matter that has been infused with enhanced life-giving properties and can therefore enliven the mineral earth.

What is farmyard manure? It is what entered as food into the animal and was received and assimilated up to a certain point by the organism. It gave occasion for the development of dynamic forces and influences in the organism, but was not primarily used to enrich the organism with material substance. It was, on the contrary, excreted. Nevertheless, it has been inside the organism and has thus been permeated with an astral and etheric content.[37] In the astral it has been permeated with nitrogen-carrying forces, and in the etheric with oxygen-carrying forces. The mass that emerges as dung is permeated with all this, and now we take it and spread it on the soil.

In doing so we are really giving the earth something etheric and astral which by rights exists in the animal's belly and there engenders plantlike forces. For the forces created in our digestive tract are plantlike in nature. We ought to be very thankful that the dung remains at all, for it carries astral and etheric contents from the interior of organs out into the open. The astral and etheric adheres to it. We only have to preserve it and use it in the right way ... Manure has enough force to overcome even the inorganic earth element.

Enhancing manure to invigorate the soil

As well as using manure as a 'given', Steiner conceived extremely practical ways—which have since been widely tried and tested, and found to be highly effective—of increasing manure's fertility-enhancing properties. Some of these methods may sound like latter-day sorcery, but Steiner is at pains to explain the rationale underlying them. And the proof of the pudding, of course, is in the eating.

A cow ... has horns to send the formative astral and etheric forces back into its digestive systems, so that much work can be accomplished there by means of these radiations from horns and hoofs ... There is something inherent in a horn that makes it well suited for reflecting living and astral influences back into the activity of the animal's interior. In a horn you have something that can radiate life and even astrality ...

This all suggests measures we might introduce to enhance the effectiveness of ordinary farm manure ...

Now, what we put into the ground, of course, must lose the form it originally had before it was consumed as fodder; it must have passed through an internal organic process in the animal's metabolic system. To a certain extent it will already have begun to decay and dissolve, but it is best if it has just reached the point where it starts to fall apart by virtue of its own etheric and astral forces. Then microscopic parasites, the smallest living creatures, put in an appearance and find a fertile breeding ground in the manure...

Next let us take the manure, in whatever form is available, and fill a cow's horn with it, then bury it in the ground at a certain depth—I would say between $\frac{3}{4}$ and $1\frac{1}{2}$ metres, provided the soil beneath is neither too clayey nor sandy... Because the cow horn is now surrounded by earth, all the earth's etherizing and astralizing energies stream into its inner cavity. The manure inside the horn attracts these forces and is inwardly enlivened by them. If the horn is buried for the entire winter—the season when the earth is most inwardly alive—all this life will be collected in the manure, turning the contents of the horn into an extremely concentrated, enlivening and fertilizing force.

Once the winter is over we can dig up the horn and remove the manure... After spending the winter underground the cow horn manure contains an immense astral and etheric energy, which you can now use by diluting the contents with ordinary water, which should perhaps be warmed a little...

To treat an area as large, say, as from the third window here to the first footpath,[38] you only need one hornful of manure diluted in about half a bucket of water. You must make sure, though, that the entire contents of the horn have been thoroughly exposed to the water. To do this, start stirring it quickly around the edge of the bucket, at the periphery, until a vortex forms that reaches nearly to the bottom, so that everything is rotating rapidly. Then reverse the direction quickly so that everything seethes and starts to swirl in the other direction. Go on mixing like this for an hour.

The next thing to do is to spray the mixture over your ploughed fields, so that it can really unite with the soil... If you manage to supplement your usual manuring with this kind of 'spiritualized manure' you will soon be struck by the enhanced fertility...

You see, these things are derived from a wider field of observation, and not just from dealing with the single thing in question—which is like trying to reconstruct a whole human being from a single finger... Studies made nowadays—on 'farm productivity' and the like—are really about nothing more than how to make production as profitable as possible... The most important thing is that once produce reaches human beings its effect on human life should be as beneficial and health-giving as possible. You can raise fruits that look magnificent in the orchard or field, but they... may merely be stomach-fillers and not enhance human life. But modern science is unable to ... provide the best kind of nourishment; it simply does not know how to go about it.

In contrast, what spiritual science has to say on the subject is rooted in the whole equilibrium and interaction of nature. It is always conceived out of the totality...

Orchestrating nature's powers: the biodynamic preparations

Extract from a lecture given in Koberwitz, Silesia, on 13 June 1924

The biodynamic preparations, some of which are described below, aim to use and combine natural forces contained in living organisms to restore vitality to an inevitably depleted soil. It is not just substances that are lost in relatively intensive farming, but also the soil's energies and life forces. Merely putting dead substances (chemicals) back into the soil is not the same as using already living, natural substances which are far more closely related to life itself than mineral fertilizers. The fact that such fertilizers 'run off' the land and pollute rivers, for example, is just one indication that the soil cannot fully absorb and integrate them.

The idea that in farming we are really *exploiting* the land is quite correct. Indeed, we cannot help doing so. With all the produce we send out into the world from our farms, we are taking forces away from the earth and even from the air. These forces must somehow be restored. The manure ... must be subjected to proper treatment, so as to sufficiently quicken and vitalize the depleted soil.

Many materialistic misconceptions have arisen in relation to this. People are at pains to investigate the working of bacteria—the smallest of living entities. They ascribe to these minute creatures the virtue of preparing the right conditions and chemical relationships in the manure. They reckon first and foremost on all that the bacteria do for the manure. Brilliant, highly logical experiments have been carried out, such as inoculating the soil with bacteria. Truly brilliant! But as a rule they have not stood the test of time, for they have proved of little use.

These things, in fact, are done from a point of view for which the following is a just parallel. Here is a room; we find an extraordinary number of flies in it. Because there are so many flies, we say the room is dirty. But the room is not dirty because of the flies. On the contrary, the flies are there because the room is dirty. Nor should we clean the room by thinking up ways to increase the number of flies (imagining that they will devour the dirt more quickly) or even to diminish them, or anything of that kind. We will achieve far more by tackling the dirt itself, directly.

The same is true when we use the products of animal excretion as manure. Minute living entities occur due to processes that are inherent in dung. The presence of these creatures may therefore be an extremely useful symptom of the prevalence of particular conditions in the dung itself. But there can be no great good in inoculating the manure with them or breeding them. (Indeed, we might often do more good by combating them.) In the living realm which is so vital to agriculture we should always retain broader perspectives. We should use atomistic forms of thought as little as possible, even in relation to these minutest of creatures...

A second thing is this: materialistic tendencies have led, in modern times, to treating manure in various ways with inorganic substances—compounds or elements. Here too, however, people are learning from experience. It has no permanent value. We must be clear that as long as we try to enhance or improve the manure by mineralizing methods, we shall only succeed in enlivening the liquid element—the water. But for a firm and sound plant structure this is not enough—for no further vitalization proceeds from the water that seeps through the soil.

We must vitalize the *earth* directly, and this we cannot do by merely mineral procedures. This we can only do by working with *organic* matter, bringing it into such a condition that it is able to organize and vitalize the solid earthy element itself...

By prolonged tillage we can gradually impoverish the soil. We are, of course, constantly impoverishing it, and that is why we have to manure it. But compensation from manuring will eventually become inadequate—and this is happening today on many farms. Then we ruthlessly exploit the soil; we allow it to become permanently impoverished.

We must ensure that proper natural processes can take place again in the right way. Certain stimulant effects are the most important of all. Trace elements people think inessential are actively at work everywhere, though in the finest and most tenuous dilution.

Therefore we need to treat our manure not only as I indicated yesterday;[39] we should also subject it to a further treatment. And the point is not merely to add substances to the soil, with the idea that it needs such and such substances so as to give them to the plants. No, the point is that we should add living forces to it. Living forces are far more important for the plant than mere substances. Though we might gradually make our soil ever so rich in this or that substance, it would still be of no use for plant growth unless, through proper manuring, we endow the plant itself with the power to receive the influences which the soil contains. This is the point...

Today therefore—more as a general indication—I shall mention a few more things of a similar kind: preparations to add to the manure in minute doses, in addition to the cow-horn manure. The preparations we add to the manure will vitalize it in a way that will enable it to transmit its vitality to the soil from which the plants are springing...

We must ensure that ... carbon, hydrogen, nitrogen and sulphur come together in the right way with other substances in the organic realm, notably with *potash* salts for instance ...

Take yarrow—a plant which is generally obtainable. If there is none of it in the district, you can use the dried herb just as well. Yarrow really is a miraculous creation. No doubt every plant is so; but if you afterwards look at any other plant, you will be deeply touched by the wonder of yarrow... Yarrow is always the greatest boon, wherever it grows wild in the country—at the edges of the fields or roads, where cereals or potatoes or any other crops are growing. It should on no account be weeded out. (Needless to say, we should prevent it from settling where it becomes a nuisance—it may become a nuisance, though it is never actually harmful.)

In a word, like sympathetic people in human society, who have a favourable influence by their mere presence and not by anything they say, so yarrow, in a district where it is plentiful, works beneficially by its mere presence.

Now you can do the following. Take the same part of the yarrow which is medicinally used, that is, the upper part—the umbel-shaped inflorescence. If you have yarrow ready to hand, so much the better. Pick the fresh flowers and let them dry, but only for a short time. In fact, you don't need to let them dry much...

Now you will see again how we always remain within the living realm. Take one or two cupped handfuls of this yarrow substance, compressing it somewhat, and sew it up in the bladder of a stag. Enclose the yarrow substance as best you can in the stag's bladder, and bind it up again. Then you have a fairly compact mass of yarrow in the stag's bladder. Now hang it up throughout the summer in a place exposed as far as possible to the sunshine. When autumn comes, take it down again and bury it not very deep in the earth, and leave it there through the winter.

Thus you will have the yarrow flower ... enclosed in the bladder of the stag for a whole year, and exposed—partly above the earth, partly below—to those influences to which it is susceptible. You will find that it assumes a particular consistency during the winter.

In this form you can now keep it as long as you wish. Add the substance which you take out of the bladder to a pile of manure . . . and distribute it well. In fact, its radiating power is so strong that if you merely put it in—even if you do not distribute it much—it will influence the whole heap of manure, or liquid manure or compost. . .

The effect of this material derived from yarrow is so enlivening and refreshing that if we now use the manure thus treated, just in the way manure is ordinarily used, we can replenish and re-enliven a soil that would otherwise be depleted. We re-endow manure with the power to enliven the earth in such a way that . . . silicic acid, lead, etc., which are needed in the earth in finest homoeopathic traces, are captured.

But the question remains: why sew up yarrow in the bladder of a stag?

Here we must gain an insight into the whole process that is connected with the *bladder*. The stag is an animal most intimately related not so much to the earth but to the earth's cosmic environment. . . Therefore the stag has antlers, the functions of which I explained yesterday.[40] Now what is present in the yarrow is particularly well preserved, both in the human and in the animal organism, by the process which takes place between the kidneys and the bladder. Moreover, this process itself is dependent on the nature or consistency of the bladder. Thus, in the bladder of the stag—however thin it is in substance—we have the necessary *forces*. Unlike the former instance (the cow, which is quite different), these forces are not connected with the animal's interior. The bladder of the stag is more connected, instead, with forces of the cosmos. In fact it is almost an image of the cosmos. We thus give yarrow the power to enhance and intensify the power it already possesses, that of combining sulphur with the other substances.

In this yarrow treatment we have an absolutely fundamental method of improving manure, and at the same time of remaining within the realm of living things. We never go out of the living realm into that of inorganic chemistry. This is an important point.

Now take another example. We want to give manure the power to receive so much life into itself that it is able to transmit life to the soil out of which the plant is growing. But we must also make the manure capable of binding together the substances that are necessary for plant growth—that is, in addition to potash, also the calcium compounds. In yarrow we are mainly dealing with potassium effects. If we also wish to fix the calcium influences, we need another plant, which— if it does not enthuse us like yarrow—also contains sulphur in homoeopathic quantity and distribution, so as to attract through the sulphur the other substances that the plant needs and draw them into an organic process.

This plant is camomile (*Chamomilla officinalis*). It is not enough to say that camomile is distinguished by its strong potash and calcium contents. The facts are these. Yarrow mainly develops its sulphur-force in the potash-forming process. Hence it has sulphur in the precise proportions that are necessary to assimilate the potash. Camomile, however, also assimilates calcium. Thus it assimilates what can chiefly help to protect the plant from the harmful effects that arise when fruit is formed, keeping the plant in a healthy condition. It is a wonderful thing to see. Camomile too has a certain amount of sulphur in it, but in a different quantity because it has calcium to assimilate as well . . .

If you want to use camomile in the right way . . . you must proceed as follows.

Pick the beautiful, delicate little yellow-white heads of the flowers, and treat them as you treated the umbels of the yarrow. But now, instead of putting them in a bladder, stuff them into bovine intestines. You will not need very much . . . Instead of using these intestinal tubes as they are commonly used for making sausages, make them into another kind of sausage—fill them with the stuffing which you thus prepare from the camomile flower.

Again, this preparation need only be exposed to the influences of nature. Observe how we constantly remain within the living realm. In this case, living vitality connected as closely as possible with the earth must be allowed to work upon the substance. You should take these precious little sausages—for they are truly precious—and expose them to the earth throughout the winter. Bury them not too deep, in soil as rich as possible in humus. If possible, choose a spot where the snow will remain for a long time and where the sun will shine upon the snow, for you will thus enable cosmic, astral influences to work down through the soil onto them.

Dig them out in the springtime and keep them in the same way as before. Add them to the manure just as you did the yarrow preparation. You will get a manure with a more stable nitrogen content, and with the added virtue of stimulating the life of the soil so that the earth itself will have a wonderfully stimulating effect on plant growth. Above all, you will create more healthy plants—really more healthy—if you manure in this way than if you do not.

I know perfectly well that all this may seem utterly mad. I only ask you to remember how many things have seemed utterly mad which have nevertheless been introduced a few years later . . .

The stinging nettle is a regular jack-of-all-trades. It can do a very great deal. It too bears within it the element which incorporates the spiritual and assimilates it everywhere, i.e. sulphur. Moreover, the stinging nettle carries the radiations of potassium and calcium, and in addition it has a kind of iron radiation. These iron radiations of the nettle are almost as beneficial to nature as the iron emanations in our blood are for us. The stinging nettle does not deserve the contempt with which we often look down on it where it grows wild in nature . . . The stinging nettle is the greatest boon.

Forgive me, Count Keyserling, if I become a little local in my references now. But if ever it is necessary to rid the soil of iron, you would do well to plant stinging nettles in out-of-the-way spots. For in a certain sense the nettle plants would liberate the uppermost layers of the soil from the iron influence, because they are so fond of it and draw it into themselves. Though this might not get rid of the iron as such, it would certainly undermine the effects of the iron on plant growth in general. Hence it would undoubtedly be of great benefit to grow stinging nettles in this district. However, I only mention that in passing, to show you how important the mere presence of the stinging nettle may be for the growth of plants in the whole surrounding area.

Now, to improve your manure still more, take any stinging nettles you can get, let them fade a little, compress them slightly, and use them in this case without any bladder or intestines. You simply bury this matter in the earth. You can use a thin layer of loose peat or the like so as to protect it from direct contact with the soil. Bury it straight in the earth, but take good note of the place, so that when you afterwards dig it out again you will not be digging out plain soil. Leave it there through the winter and the following summer—it must be buried for a whole year.

This substance will now be extremely effective. Mix it with the manure, just as you did the other preparations. The general effect will be that the manure becomes inwardly sensitive—truly sensitive and sentient, we might almost say intelligent. It will not suffer any undue decomposition to take place in it—any loss of nitrogen or the like.

This 'condiment' not only makes the manure intelligent but also the soil itself—the earth into which the manure is worked. The soil will individualize itself in conformity with the particular plants you are growing. It is like infusing the soil with reason and intelligence, which you can bring about by this addition of *Urtica dioica*.

Modern methods of improving the manure may sometimes give surprising superficial results, but ultimately they tend to turn all first-rate produce into stomach ballast only. Such produce will eventually lose its nutritional qualities. You should not be deceived by the swollen size of produce. The point is that it should have real nutritional energy.

Now we may be concerned, here or there in our farming work, with the occurrence of plant diseases. I am speaking in general terms at the moment. Nowadays people are fond of specialization in all things; therefore they speak of specific diseases. It is quite right to do so ... We can perfect our descriptions of disease, we can know precisely what happens in the organism in terms of modern physiology or physiological chemistry; and yet we may still not be able to heal the disease at all. In healing we must proceed not from the histological or microscopic diagnosis, but from the great universal connections. And the same is true in relation to the plant world . . .

A large number of plant diseases, although not all, can be alleviated by improving our manuring, i.e. by the following methods. We must bring calcium into the soil via the manure. But it will not be much use to bring the calcium to the soil by any means other than the living sphere. To have a healing effect, the calcium must remain within the realm of life; it must not fall out of the living realm. Ordinary lime or the like is of no use at all in this respect.

But there is a plant containing plenty of calcium—77 per cent of the plant substance, albeit in very fine distribution. I'm thinking of the oak—in particular oak bark, which represents a kind of intermediate product between plant and living soil. Of the many forms in which calcium can appear, the calcium structure of oak bark is ideal . . .

Calcium has the property which I explained once before. It restores order when the etheric body is working too strongly, that is, when it prevents the astral gaining access to an organic entity. It 'kills off' or damps down the etheric body, and thereby liberates the influences of the astral body. All limestone does this. But if we want rampant etheric development, of whatever kind, to contract in a regular, fine manner without giving shocks to organic life, then we must use the calcium in the very structure in which we find it in the bark of the oak.

We collect oak bark. We do not need much—no more than can easily be obtained. We collect it and chop it up a little, till it has a crumblike consistency. Then we take a skull—the skull of any of our domestic animals will do, it makes little or no difference. We put the chopped-up oak bark in the skull, close it up again as well as possible with bony material and lower it into the earth, but not too deep. We cover it over with peat, and then introduce some kind of channel or water-pipe so as to let as much rainwater as possible flow into the place... This, once again, must hibernate. Water from melting snow is just as good as rainwater. It must pass through the autumn and winter in this way. Adding the resulting mass to your manure will lend it the forces to combat or arrest any harmful plant diseases.

So we have added four different things. All this requires a certain amount of work, it is true—yet if you think it over, it involves less work than all the devices that are pursued in the chemical laboratories of modern agriculture, which are also costly. You will soon see that what we have suggested here is more economical.

But we shall also need something to attract the silicic acid from the whole cosmic environment, for we must have this silicic acid in the plant. Precisely with regard to silicic acid, the earth gradually loses its power in the course of time. It loses it very slowly so that we do not notice it. Those who only look at the microcosmic level and never at macrocosmic connections are unconcerned in any case about this loss of silicic acid; they think it insignificant for the growth of plants. In reality, it is of the greatest significance...

I know that those who have studied modern agriculture will say that I have not yet told you how to improve the manure's nitrogen content. On the contrary, I have been speaking of it all the time, in relation to yarrow, camomile and stinging nettle. For there is a hidden alchemy in the organic process. This hidden alchemy really transmutes the potash, for example, into nitrogen, provided only that the potash is working properly in the organic process. It even transforms lime into nitrogen if it is working properly. In the growth of plants all the four elements of which I have been speaking are involved. Hydrogen is also there, in addition to sulphur. I have told you of the significance of hydrogen. Now there is a mutual and qualitative relationship between the calcium/lime and the hydrogen, similar to that between oxygen and nitrogen in the air.

Even a quantitative chemical analysis might be able to reveal the relationship between the oxygen and nitrogen in the air and the lime and hydrogen in organic processes. The fact is that under the influence of hydrogen, lime and potash are constantly being transmuted into something resembling nitrogen, and at length into actual nitrogen. And the nitrogen which is formed in this way is of the greatest benefit to plant growth, but we must allow it to be produced by the methods I have described . . .

Silicic acid is needed to draw in cosmic influences, and a thorough interaction must come about between the silicic acid and the potassium in a plant . . . We must now look for a plant whose own potassium-silicic acid relationship can impart to the dung—again, if added to it in a kind of homoeopathic dose—the corresponding power. And we can find it. This, too, is a plant which it is already beneficial to have just growing on our farm—the common dandelion (*Taraxacum officinale*).

The innocent yellow dandelion is a tremendous asset because it mediates between silicic acid finely, homoeo-pathically distributed in the cosmos, and what is needed as silicic acid in the soil. The dandelion is a kind of messenger from heaven. But if we want to make it effective in the manure we must use it in the right way. To this end—it will almost go without saying by now—we must expose the dandelion to the influences of the earth, in the winter season.

Gather the yellow heads of the dandelion and let them fade a little. Pack them together, sew them up in a bovine mesentery, and lay them in the earth throughout the winter.

When these balls are dug up in the spring you can keep them until you need them. They are now thoroughly saturated with cosmic influences. The substance you get out of them can once again be added to the dung, and in a similar way. This will give the soil the capacity to attract as much silicic acid from the atmosphere and from the cosmos as the plants need to make them really sensitive and responsive to all that is at work in their environment, and then they themselves will be able to draw in whatever else they need.

To be able to grow properly, plants must have a kind of sensitivity. Even as I, a human being, can pass a dull fellow by and he will not notice me, so too all that is in the soil and above it will pass a dull plant by and the plant will fail to sense it; it will not, therefore, enlist it in the service of its growth. But if the plant is thus finely permeated and vitalized with silicic acid, it will grow sensitive to all things, and will draw to itself all that it needs.

Even plants, in order to grow properly, need to have a certain ability to sense and perceive . . . We can easily weaken a plant so that it only takes advantage of what is present in its immediate environment. But it is not good to do so. Treat the soil as I have now described, and the plant will be prepared to draw things to itself from a wide circle. Your plant will then benefit not only from what is in the tilled field itself, where it grows, but also from what is in the soil of an adjacent meadow, or of a neighbouring wood or forest. That is what happens, once it has thus become inwardly sensitive. We can bring about a wonderful interplay in nature, by giving plants the forces which the dandelion makes available to them in this way.

And so I think you should try to create good fertilizers by enriching your manure with these five ingredients—or suitable substitutes. Manure in future should not be treated with all manner of chemicals, but with these five: yarrow, camomile, stinging nettle, oak bark and dandelion. Such a manure will contain a great deal of what is actually needed.

Now there is one more thing you can do. Before you make use of the manure prepared in this way, press the blossoms from the valerian plant (*Valeriana officinalis*) and greatly dilute the extract with warm water. You can do this at any time and store it. If this diluted valerian juice is applied to the manure in very fine distribution, it will stimulate it to relate in the right way to phosphorus.

With the help of these six ingredients you can produce an excellent fertilizer—whether from liquid manure, ordinary farmyard manure or compost.

29. The Meditating Farmer

Extract from a lecture given in Koberwitz, Silesia, on
11 June 1924

*To end Part Seven here is a brief but vital extract, in which Steiner
as it were hands back to the farmer full responsibility for deciding
what the land and its crops need. If instead of relying on directives
from experts—or even a whole European Community—we
develop an intimate, meditative relationship with our particular
farm and its environment, the right ideas and inspirations can
arise, and the farmer can become what he or she should be: the
farm's living consciousness and conscience.*

You see, if you bump your head against something hard—a
table, for instance—you will only be aware of your own pain.
If however you rub against it more gently, you will become
aware of the surface of the table, its texture and so on. It is the
same when you meditate. You gradually grow into an
experience of, for instance, the nitrogen that surrounds
you . . .

And in fact it is at this point that the spirit in our inner,
meditative activity begins to acquire a certain relationship to
farming . . . It is not a bad thing, you know, when a farmer can
meditate and thus become ever more receptive to the reve-
lations of nitrogen. Our agricultural practices will gradually
change once we become receptive to what nitrogen can
reveal. Suddenly we know all kinds of things—they are
simply there. Suddenly we know all about the mysteries at
work on the land and around the farm . . . Take a simple

farmer ... who meditates on all sorts of things during the winter nights. And indeed he arrives at a way of acquiring spiritual knowledge, though he may not be able to express it ... As he is walking through the fields it is suddenly there. He knows what to do, and he tries it out. I lived among farmers when I was young, and I saw this happen again and again. It really does happen.

These are the kinds of things we have to pursue. Mere intellectualism is not enough; it does not take us deep enough. Nature's life and flow are so fine and subtle that in the end they slip right through the coarse mesh of our rational concepts. That's the mistake science has made in recent times—it tries to use coarse conceptual nets to catch things that are actually much too fine for them ...

Part Eight:

REAPING THE WHIRLWIND

30. Exploiting Nature: Economy Versus Ecology

The extracts which follow focus on the whole uneasy relationship between ecology and economics in humanity's relationship to nature. Where economic factors take precedence over care for the natural world, leading to practices that override the health of plants and animals, short-term gain is bought at the cost of long-term degeneration and ultimately disaster.

Exploitation weakens natural forces

Extract from a lecture given in Dornach on
5 December 1923

Artificially increasing yields to meet short-term needs may seem economically viable or even vital, but when set against the long-term damage to animals over many generations this is not only counter-productive but counter to nature, and will reap unsustainably harmful consequences.

I can tell you, for example, that as a boy I had numerous personal experiences relating to beekeeping, and at that time my interest in this matter was very great—not because of any connection beekeeping had to economic or commercial questions that interested me after I grew up, but rather because honey was prohibitively expensive at that time so that my parents, who were poor, could never afford to buy any. Whatever honey we had came from our neighbours, usually for Christmas, but we received so much throughout the winter that we had enough honey for the entire year. At that time I wasn't interested in the economic question relating to honey, since I ate honey almost exclusively given as a gift. Why was this? Nowadays people are less likely to receive honey as a present. But back then, in the area where my parents lived, the beekeepers were mainly farmers who included beekeeping in their whole agricultural practice.

This is quite a different situation from someone setting up as a beekeeper and buying whatever he needs for this ... and such a person having to live entirely from hourly wages. When included as part of the farm, beekeeping is carried on in such a way that you hardly notice it. Scarcely any consideration is even given to the length of time spent on this activity because it is something the farmer somehow manages to find time to do ... The hives were tended as just one of the other chores in those days, and people knew that honey was something so valuable you couldn't even pay for it. And in a certain sense this is absolutely right because, under today's economic conditions, everything you can buy suffers from an improper relationship between price and the actual work done ... if the organization of a society were a healthy one, then a proper price for honey would doubtless arise.

It is precisely because we are not living under healthy social conditions that all the questions we raise will be tainted by the situation we are part of. You see, here is the situation today when you visit large farms. Yes gentlemen, what the agricultural manager—usually not even a farmer but an accountant-type manager—will tell you about the quantity of milk obtained from cows is terrible. The manager reckons on so many litres of milk a day from each cow. Anyone who really understands the nature of a cow knows that it is impossible to get this much milk from a cow. But somehow they manage it. As far as I know, some of them have pushed up the amount to double what a cow can normally give. Naturally this brings in a good profit for the farm. And ... you can't even say you can tell that the milk doesn't have the same nutritional value as milk produced under natural conditions. You can't even prove anything bad has happened to it.

But let me give the following example. Over the past few years we have done many experiments with a medication used to treat foot-and-mouth disease in cattle.[41] These experiments were conducted on large farms as well as small ones, where milk production for each cow was lower... These experiments were never completed because, officially, people did not want to comply with all the aspects involved and because so many concessions have to be made nowadays. But the medication produced some extraordinary results. In a somewhat altered form this remedy is now used to treat canine distemper.

When you do these experiments you discover the following. Calves born to cows that produce too much milk are considerably weaker. You can observe this in the effect the medication has on the calf. The effectiveness or lack of it is greatly magnified. Eventually the calf grows up if it doesn't die of the disease. But a calf whose mother has been overfed in order to force it to give more milk is a much weaker calf than one whose mother was not forced to produce as much milk. You can observe this in the first, second, third and fourth generations ... I am fully aware that if people continue like this, if a single cow is made to produce over 30 litres of milk a day, if they go on being mistreated like this, then dairy farming will eventually come to a bitter end ...

Mad cows

Extract from a lecture given in Dornach on 13 January 1923

Another prescient insight by Steiner, which, less than a hundred years after he spoke these words, did indeed prove true. As we now know, cows fed meat can go on to develop 'mad cow disease'.

You know that there are some animals that are simply gentle, vegetarian creatures and do not eat meat. Cows, for example, don't eat meat. Nor do horses eat meat, but only plants...

Consider an ox or cow... the ox itself produces the flesh in its body from plant substances... This animal's body can therefore produce meat from plants. Now you can cook cabbage for as long as you like and it won't turn into meat! You do not produce meat in your frying pan or stew pot, and nobody has ever baked a cake that became meat... Yet the animal can accomplish inwardly what one can't do outwardly. Flesh is produced in the animal's body, and forces to do this must first be present in the body. With all our technological advances we have no technology that can produce meat from plants. We can't do this, but in our bodies and in animal bodies there are forces that can make meat substance from plant substance...

Now imagine that an ox suddenly decided that it was too tiresome to graze and nibble plants, that it would let another animal eat them and do the work for it, and then it would eat the animal. In other words, the ox would begin to eat meat, although it can produce flesh by itself, having the inner forces to do so. What would happen if the ox were to eat meat directly instead of plants? He would leave unused all the forces that can produce flesh in him from plants. Think of the tremendous amount of energy lost when the machines in a factory where something or other is manufactured are all turned on without producing anything. There is a tremendous waste of energy. But the unused energy in the ox's body simply cannot be lost, so the ox will ultimately be filled with it, and this pent-up force does something in him other than produce flesh from plant substances... After all, the energy remains and is present in the animal, and thus makes waste products. Instead of ox flesh, harmful substances are produced. If an ox were suddenly to start eating meat, therefore, it would fill itself with all kinds of harmful substances such as uric acid and urates.

Now urates have their specific effects. The specific effects of urates are expressed in a particular affinity for the nervous system and the brain. This means that if an ox were to consume meat directly, large amounts of urates would be secreted and enter the ox's brain, making him go crazy. If an experiment could be conducted in which a herd of oxen were suddenly fed with pigeons, it would produce a completely mad herd... The oxen would turn into terribly wild, furious creatures...

Battery farming

Extract from a lecture given in Koberwitz, Silesia, on 16 June 1924

Not only are cramped or even battery conditions appalling treatment to inflict on other sentient beings, but this, says Steiner, will also have a dire effect on future generations of livestock.

It is important not to keep animals confined in dark stalls where no cosmic forces can reach them, but to let them out to pasture and give them opportunities to interact with their surroundings through their senses. Just picture an animal in some dark, airless building, standing before a feeding trough that contains whatever a human being thinks fit. If it never has the opportunity to be outdoors this animal will be very different from one which can roam freely and use its senses— its sense of smell for instance—to seek out cosmic forces. It will be very different from an animal that actively forages for its own food. The animal penned in front of the trough will not immediately show its lack of cosmic forces, for it still inherits some, but this deficiency will gradually become apparent in its descendants. These animals will become weak because of their head, they will be unable to properly nourish their bodies because they will be unable to absorb the cosmic influences which their bodies require. These things will show you that what is important is not to come up with generalities about what to feed in this or that instance, but rather to understand what value particular feeding methods have for the animal's whole nature and constitution.

Notes from a conversation between Rudolf Steiner and the chemist Johann Simon Streicher, on 9 October 1920

The extravagant praise for stall feeding in recent years is certainly connected with the incidence of tuberculosis among cattle, and also with the fact that although animals may produce more milk or whatever for a while, their state of health will inevitably decline over generations. Even manure collected from a pasture by someone with a basket on their back and a shovel in hand is undoubtedly better than the manure which comes from stall feeding. It is harmful for animals to absorb the breath of a neighbouring animal while they are feeding. On the pastures you will find that animals always keep a certain distance from one another ... they space themselves at considerable distances because they cannot abide the breath of neighbouring animals while they're feeding.

31. A Mechanized Civilization

Not only do we use machines, but machines work back upon us, altering our outlook and mode of engagement with the world. Any reasonably sensitive person who has spent much time in front of a computer can testify to its potentially deadening effects—if not in some way consciously counteracted—on individual human creativity. It starts to be harder, as Steiner says here, to 'feel human'. At the same time this mechanization of consciousness will inevitably impact on our sensitivity towards subtle processes and interactions in the natural world. But besides weakening our relationship with natural phenomena, human-produced electrical frequencies in the atmosphere—from mobile phones etc.—may also weaken or disrupt aspects of the actual physical substance which constitutes us and the rest of nature. Two—as yet not wholly proven—examples will have to suffice here: the suspected impact on the brain from mobile phone use, and the fact that bee colonies seem to be disturbed and even to disappear altogether in response to wireless broadband radiation. This is a huge field for research, and one clearly that had not fully begun to impact on the world in 1923. Nevertheless, Steiner here too seems to have some prescient inklings.

Extract from a lecture given in Dornach on
20 October 1923

We are now living in an age when the evolution of the world is threatened by a certain danger ... of one-sided influences coming to one-sided expression in people... The following could happen. Over recent centuries technology, an external technological approach to things, has developed under the influence of external science. Certainly, our technical progress is wonderful in every sphere. The forces of nature are active in technology in their lifeless form. And the important factors in bringing these lifeless forces into play so absolutely and utterly that they inform civilization throughout the earth are number, measure and weight.

The scales, the measuring rod—to weigh, count and measure—these are the ideal of the modern scientist and technician...

At present, machines are still imperfect and primitive, but everything is tending towards the gradual development of a kind of machine that depends on oscillation, in which oscillation, vibration and sequential motion produce the machine's effect. Everything is tending towards such machines. But if [such] machines can be constructed ... then the oscillations produced by them would ... compel the motions of our planetary system to resonate with the earth, just as a string tuned to a certain pitch vibrates in sympathy when another is struck in the same room... Human civilization would resound with the clattering and rattling which would stream down to earth from the cosmos as a reaction to this mechanization of the earth.

If you observe what is happening nowadays, you can say that modern civilization is actually on the way to making this terrible, degenerative aspect its goal... We need to learn not only about earth's gravity, not merely to weigh, measure and count ... but also turn our gaze to the heights so that what would otherwise become a purely mechanized civilization can be spiritualized...

Extract from a lecture given in Dornach on
25 November 1917

I have often pointed out ... that human consciousness is
linked with the forces of destruction... These death forces
will grow ever stronger. Connections will be created
between the human being's death energies—which are
related to electrical and magnetic forces—and external
mechanical forces. People will become able to steer their
intentions and thoughts in a certain way into these
mechanical forces...

A [further] thing will be the intervention of human thought
into how the human race comes about through birth and
conception... In the future, materialistic science will inter-
vene in conception and the way male and female are har-
nessed together...[42]

From [the West] will come endeavours to make use of
something that can work through the most material of
forces... More than anything else, that quarter will strive to
make use of electricity, especially the earth's magnetism, to
induce effects all over the world...

Extract from a discussion held in Koberwitz, Silesia, on
16 June 1924

Question: *Is it permissible to preserve bulk fodder by means of
electric currents?*

Steiner: What do you hope to accomplish by that? Here of course the whole role of electricity in nature needs to be considered. It is of some comfort to know that at least in America, where people are developing a better gift for observation than here in Europe, voices can be heard saying that human beings will no longer be able to grow and develop as they used to, now that the whole atmosphere has electric currents and radiations running through it. This has an effect on the whole development of the human being. It even makes a difference whether the trains in a particular area have steam engines or are electrified. The effects of steam can be recognized, but electricity has a terribly unconscious way of working—people simply cannot tell where certain influences are coming from ... Electricity gradually erases comprehension and this effect is already noticeable today; you can already see that people have a harder time understanding things they encounter than they did a few decades ago ...

You mustn't forget that electricity always works more strongly on the head organization of humans and animals (and correspondingly on the root organization of plants). If you preserve fodder by passing electric current through it, the animals that eat this will eventually become sclerotic. This is a slow process—you won't notice it straight away. You might notice at first that the animals tend to die sooner than they ought to, but you'll blame it on all kinds of other things ... electricity is really not something that can work on living things in any beneficial way. You see, electricity lies at one level below living things ... if you continually force an organism to defend itself unnecessarily against such an influence, it will gradually become nervous, fidgety and sclerotic ...

Extract from a lecture given in Stuttgart on 11 July 1923

In times when there were no electrical currents, when the air was not swarming with electrical influences, it was easier to be human . . . For this reason, in order to be human at all today, one has to expend much stronger spiritual capacities than was necessary a century ago.

But I have no wish to be conservative and say that we should banish all these scientific advances. No. Modern human beings need the access to the spirit that spiritual science provides, so that through this strong experience of the spirit they can also become stronger in relation to the forces that accompany modern culture, the forces that harden our physical body and deprive us of its responsiveness.

32. Natural Catastrophes: Weather, Climate and Earthquakes

Tsunamis, floods, whirlwinds, melting glaciers and natural disasters of all kinds are increasingly the daily fare of newspapers, as climate change and global warming advances in seemingly inexorable fashion. There was little of this to be heard in the 1920s, certainly not as a pressing concern of humanity; yet Steiner draws subtle connections between weather phenomena, volcanic eruptions or natural disasters and human morality. We are a part of the natural world and our conduct, for good or ill, has a direct impact on it.

Extract from a lecture given in Dornach on 30 July 1916

Here Steiner identifies two kinds of natural phenomena: predictable ones which recur reliably, and much more haphazard ones such as weather, storms and volcanic eruptions. But these, or something closely related to them, also exist in the human being. Thus we are closely connected with the weather through our own nature—and it is only a small step from there, though Steiner does not yet mention this in the passage below, to a possibility that we might also affect it.

Today I would like to begin by considering a simple fact of which everyone is aware. If we cast an understanding and observant eye over the variety of natural occurrences, we will notice that they seem to fall into two very different and distinct realms: one realm which manifests the greatest kind of regularity and order, and another realm of extensive disorder, irregularity and virtually impenetrable interconnections. This, at any rate, is how we experience them. Even though there is a sharp dividing line between these two realms, our normal sciences do not distinguish clearly between them.

On the one hand we have all the things that happen with the regularity with which the sun rises and sets each morning and evening, and with which the stars rise and set, and with which all the other things associated with the rising and setting of the sun occur—such as the plants, which regularly sprout and grow in the spring, develop through the summer, then fade away and disappear in autumn. And the realm of nature presents us with many other things in which we can see a similar degree of regularity and order.

But there is another realm of nature, one which cannot be experienced in the same way. One cannot predict storms in the way one can anticipate the sunrise and sunset each morning and evening, for storms do not occur with that kind of regularity. We can say that the sun will occupy a certain position in the heavens at ten o'clock tomorrow morning. But we cannot say that we will see a certain cloud formation in a certain position, let alone say anything about how the clouds will look. Nor can we predict, in the way we can predict the quarters of the moon, that here in our building in Dornach we are going to be surprised by a storm or shower at some particular time. It is possible to calculate eclipses of the sun and moon that will happen centuries hence quite accurately, but the occurrence of earthquakes and volcanic eruptions cannot be predicted with anything like the same degree of certainty.

You see here two distinct realms of nature, one that

manifests regularities our reason can grasp, and the other whose manifestations are irregular and cannot be experienced in the same way. Great regularity and extreme unpredictability are intertwined in nature as a whole. I would like to describe the overall impression that nature makes on us at a given instant as a mixture of the orderly procession of regular events with those other events, the ones that can take us by surprise, even though they recur repeatedly with at least a certain degree of consistency.

There is a profound truth that we have considered from many points of view in the course of our studies here: that the human being is a microcosm—that we mirror the macrocosm and that everything found at large there can be rediscovered in some form in ourselves. So we would expect to find these two spheres of nature expressed in some human form, one which exhibits great order, the other which exhibits great irregularity. Naturally, in a human life these would be expressed very differently from the way they are expressed externally in nature. Nevertheless, that twofold division of nature into order and irregularity should remind us of something in ourselves.

Now consider the typical example I tried to present to you yesterday. The person I mentioned[43] was perfectly able to think logically. When it was a matter of logical thinking, he could calculate, pass judgements and regulate his life with a degree of order, overseeing it and planning and acting accordingly. In other words, he had access to everything that regularity can contribute to the functioning of our understanding, our reason, our capacity for experience and our will impulses. But, alongside these, this person also lived another life, a life that was expressed in those two works I described to you. From the little I have told you about the content of these books you can well imagine how stormy a life this was, how erratic when compared with what human reason has to offer. There were storms in the depths of that soul, profound storms, and these storms were lived out in the way we described yesterday. Such things truly do happen in the way thunderstorms and outbursts of wind and weather play into the regular procession of sun and moon, into the orderly succession of sprouting, fading away and dying in the plant world. Into all that develops out of the human head and the regular course of the human heart erupt the storms we experience as waking dreams or as lightning flashes of genius. These flash through the soul and discharge themselves like storms. But be in no doubt about it, every human soul has the tendency to experience the very same things that Otto Weininger experienced in such an extreme, radically para-doxical fashion. They are there in the depths of every human soul.

Extract from a lecture given in London on 16 November 1922

Spiritual beings—which Steiner calls 'luciferic' and 'ahrimanic'— live in various natural phenomena. The former try to draw us away from fully conscious, earthly presence of mind, and are embodied in all fluctuations of weather; the latter, which seek to immerse us in matter and blind physicality, find expression in volcanic eruption and earthquakes. This might seem to absolve us of responsibility for such phenomena, but the opposite is the case. Such beings are intimately linked with us, and our moral balance or lack of it gives them greater power to wrest the natural order out of equilibrium.

The supersensible nature that is around us can be understood and appreciated only by someone who has developed spiritual insight, and who does not continually focus, as science does today, on the strict dictates of purely natural, material laws . . . The supersensible realities that underlie external nature will never reveal themselves to such research. However, they will become evident if we learn to look with keen and discerning spiritual vision upon things which natural law cannot wholly explain, but are generally regarded as subject to chance.

Of this character are the phenomena of the weather, all the irregularities of the atmosphere throughout the four seasons of the year. If you stop to consider in detail, for example, how a London fog arises,[44] you may find that its arrival is based on certain causes. You will not, however, be able to trace all its continual changes and movements. When it comes to the particular, changing phenomena of wind and weather, we are inclined to say that we are at the mercy of chance. You can of course read in the newspapers a forecast of what kind of weather we are likely to have in the near future, but you will not depend on it with the same certainty with which you rely on the sun rising tomorrow morning. Phenomena which show the working of natural law are in quite another category from the phenomena of wind and weather, which are more or less generally ascribed to the working of so many chance factors. People can and do acquire a certain prophetic gift but this cannot be ascribed a validity within the framework of natural law.

As a matter of fact, beings live in all the various manifestations of wind and weather—beings whom we do not see only because they lack a body visible to the senses. They are present and alive, nevertheless. The beings who live in wind and weather have a body that consists of air and warmth, a body that has in it no water—no fluidity, that is, of any kind— and no solid earth; it consists of nothing but air and warmth. And this body is continually undergoing sudden changes. At one moment it will assume form and shape, then again it will dissolve and pass away. The changing cloud formations that we observe in the sky, the play of the currents of the wind: these are not the body—which remains more hidden—but are the outer expression, the deeds, of the beings of whom I speak. When therefore we look out into the atmosphere which surrounds our earth, and within which we ourselves are living, we have there around us a world of beings composed merely of air and warmth. They are the same kind as those whom I have called in my books and frequently spoken of in lectures as luciferic beings.

Now these beings have a specific end in view in regard to us human beings. Notwithstanding the fact that they inhabit an element which we often find far from agreeable and pleasant— living, as we have said, in the weather!—these beings attach great value to the moral element in the human social order. So highly do they prize it that in their opinion it would be best for us not to have a physical body at all—not, at any rate, a body that partakes of the watery or earthly elements. If they could have formed us in their own way, they would have made us moral beings, pure and simple. In this case, of course, we would not have had freedom; we would have been moral without being inwardly free. As it is, these beings wage a fearful battle in the course of the year, struggling to wrest us away from the earth and draw us into their own sphere. They would like to draw us away from the earth—make us strangers to it. This is why they are particularly dangerous for people inclined to any kind of visionary idealism or vague mysticism. Such people readily fall prey to these beings who seek to entice us away from the earth and endow us with a kind of angelic nature, so that under no circumstances would we find ourselves tempted to be other than purely moral.

Strange therefore and paradoxical as it may sound, dear friends, inhabiting the forces that pulsate through the encircling air in all the vagaries of wind and weather are beings who, abhorring human freedom and desiring nothing better than its complete annihilation, want to make the human being into a moral automaton, want to make him a kind of good angel. And they fight hard to attain their end; to use an earthly expression, they wage war to do so.

In addition to these beings who build, as it were, their strongholds in the air—I am obliged to speak in pictures—there are also beings of a contrary nature, to whom I alluded in my last lecture in another connection. And this latter class of beings has to do with all that comes to expression in our instinctive urges and impulses, in our desires and passions. You must not however think of them as belonging first and foremost to the human being. Within ourselves we can see the results of their activity. But they have their home, so to speak, on and within the earth itself. Only we cannot see them, for these beings too do not have a body visible to us. They have, in fact, a body that lives entirely in the elements of earth and water. And their deeds are to be seen in the ebb and flow of the tides, in volcanic eruptions and in earthquakes. Science, as we know, can find no fully satisfactory explanation for these phenomena...

Now, these ahrimanic powers also cherish a particular aim

as regards the human being. With the help of their various sub-spirits, which inhabit the earth and its water elements and can, for example, be recognized even in the sprites or brownies of fairy lore, the ahrimanic powers aim to carry out another and a different project . . .

These other beings build their strongholds immediately below the surface of the earth, and their activities rise up into our metabolism—for the phenomena we observe in the tides and less frequently in volcanic eruptions and earthquakes are always present also in the ebb and flow of our metabolism. Whilst the luciferic spirits build, as we said, their strongholds in the air, in order to fight for the moral—as against the earthly—element in the human being, the ahrimanic beings struggle to harden us; they want to make us like themselves. Were they to be successful, we would become extremely clever in the material realm—incredibly clever and intelligent. They cannot achieve their end directly, but they aim at doing so indirectly . . .

We have thus around us in our earthly environment two hosts of beings: those in the air who want to make us moral but also to lift us away from the earth; and then also, immediately below the surface of the earth, the ahrimanic beings who want to draw us down and chain us permanently to the earth . . .

Extract from a lecture given in Paris on 12 June 1906

Now Steiner makes a direct link between natural cataclysms—both in the long-distant past and in the present—and forces at work in the human being.

Underneath the solid earth there are a large number of subterranean spaces which communicate with the sixth layer, that of fire.[45] This element of the fire-earth is intimately connected with the human will. It is this element which produced the tremendous eruptions that brought the Lemurian epoch[46] to an end. At that time the forces which nourish the human will went through a trial which unleashed the fire catastrophe that destroyed the Lemurian continent. In the course of evolution this sixth layer receded more and more toward the centre, and as a result volcanic eruptions became less frequent. And yet they are still produced as a result of the human will which, when it is evil and chaotic, magnetically acts on this layer and disrupts it.

Nevertheless, when the human will is devoid of egotism, it is able to appease this fire. Materialistic periods are mostly accompanied and followed by natural cataclysms, earthquakes, etc. Growing powers of evolution are the only alchemy capable of transforming, little by little, the organism and the soul of the earth.

Extract from a lecture given in Berlin on 1 January 1909

Here, interestingly, Steiner seems to draw an oblique parallel between human-induced cataclysms in ancient times and our modern carbon-emitting industries. He specifically identifies a human impact on the climate and weather phenomena, and earthquakes.

In Atlantean times the seminal forces in plant and animal were still under the human being's control and could be drawn forth just as the forces used in the form of steam for propelling machines can be extracted from mineral coal today. I have told you that when these forces are drawn forth they are connected in a mysterious way with nature forces in wind, weather and the like; and if used by human beings for purposes counter to divine purposes, these nature forces are called into action against them.

Here lies the cause of the Atlantean flood and of the devastation wrought by the powers of nature which led to the disappearance of the whole continent of Atlantis...

What manifests in the phenomena of outer nature, in air and water, in cloud formations, in lightning and thunder—all this is, so to speak, a last vestige on the earth's surface of [ancient] forces... By what is working in these forces, the earth's inner fire energies are placed at the service of Ahriman.[47] There he has the centre of his activity; and whereas his spiritual influences make their way to human souls and lead them to error, we see how Ahriman—in a certain respect shackled—has certain foci for his activity in the interior of the earth. Were we to understand the mysterious effects of Ahriman's influence ... we should recognize in the quakes and tremors of the earth the connection between such grievous, tragic happenings in nature and the sway of earthly powers...

In a certain sense we can recognize an echoing of these fire forces, which in earlier times were withdrawn from the human being's control, in what is wrought by fire in such terrible manifestations of nature...

There we see a connection which seems to be like a relic of catastrophes undergone by humanity in the far distant past... The forces working through air and water led, via human passions, to the Atlantean catastrophes. These catastrophes were evoked by the collective karma[48] of humanity, but a relic has remained and this relic awakens the echoes of those earlier catastrophes. Our volcanic eruptions and earthquakes are nothing else than the echoes of these catastrophes.

Part Nine:

LIFTING THE CHALICE

33. The Cosmos Within

Coming full circle we return to the human being: to our capacity, or lack of it, to engage fully with the fragile earth; to understand it in heart and body as well as mind. Steiner's reiteration of the word 'head' in the passage below reminds me of the headlike computer through which so many of us nowadays 'connect' with every-thing—but in very abstract and often superficial ways. Without relinquishing a hard-won sense of self, which can be the only basis for ecological responsibility, we can still learn to live more in tune with Creation.

Extract from a lecture given in Stuttgart on 13 October 1922

The human being who is growing into the epoch of the consciousness soul[49] is today locked in the head's abstract ideas. But outside our head, if I may so express myself, lives the desire to experience more than the head is able to. To begin we only have a connection with nature formed between her and our head. Everything we understand through science, so far as we consider it valid, is acquired from nature through the head. Nowadays the abstract head continually interposes itself between us and nature. It is as though everything that comes to the human being from the world were to pour itself into the head, as though the head were entirely choked up so that it lets nothing through its dense layers that could bring about a relation with the world. Everything remains stuck fast in the head . . . But we cannot, in fact, live merely as a head, for joined to it is the rest of the organism. The life of the rest of the organism remains dull, unconscious, because everything is directed towards the head. Everything stops short there . . .

The head has gradually become an insatiable glutton, wanting everything that comes from the world outside to pass through it; and, as far as our heart and the rest of our organism is concerned, we are obliged to live as if we had no real connection with the surrounding world.

But these other parts of the organism develop wish, will, capacity for desire. They feel isolated. For instance, the eyes catch colours and only scanty remains of these are experienced in the head, so that the colours cannot work right through us, they cannot reach the blood or the nervous system in the rest of the body. It is only in our head that we still know something about the world. But all the greater is the intense desire of the rest of the organism to connect with the outside world. This desire lives in the evolving human being: a desire to find some kind of connection with the world not only through the head but the rest of the organism; to learn to think not only with the head but with our whole organism; to learn to experience the world with every part of us and not just the head.

Extract from a lecture given in Oslo at Whitsun 1923

The following vision—no less a word will do—of the vast worlds contained in the human being, reflecting the vast worlds surrounding us, can summon up a sense of awe of a kind that underlies all deep ecological thinking.

We see marvellous sights when admiring a beautiful landscape, marvellous sights when admiring the starry sky at night in all its splendour. Yet in viewing a human lung, a human liver, not with the anatomist's physical eye but with the eye of spirit, we see whole worlds compressed into a small space. Apart from the splendour and glory of all the rivers and mountains on the surface of the earth, a still more exalted splendour adorns what lies within our skin, even in its merely physical aspect. It is irrelevant that all this is of smaller scale than the seemingly vast world of space. If you survey what lies in a single pulmonary vesicle, it will appear as more grandiose than the whole range of the mighty Alps. For what lies inside the human being is the whole spiritual cosmos in condensed form. In our inner organism we have an image of the entire cosmos.

34. Warming the Globe with Compassion

Extract from a lecture given in Prague on 28 March 1911

The meaning of human evolution, and the evolution of the earth so closely connected with it, is to develop in us the warmth of love and compassion. Our organism is the substance, like the wax of a candle, which can be transformed into light. Though Steiner does not state this explicitly here in this powerful, uplifting passage, it seems to me that the reverse might also be true: that the warmth and heat we do not transform into compassion for the natural world—out of which we grow, which sustains us, and which as a more 'adult' humanity we can care for responsibly—might 'fall back' a level and manifest as the physical heat of global warming. This, certainly, is the challenge we now face: either to develop the transformed 'blossom' of compassion, and realize this in active, responsible deeds in so many spheres of life, or to be submerged by the harmful environmental effects of human egotism and short-sightedness.

What the organism produces in the way of inner warmth processes in our blood, warmth processes which it conducts to us through all its different processes, and which it finally brings to expression in a flowering of all other processes, penetrates up into the soul and spirit, transforms itself into soul and spirit. The most beautiful, the loftiest thing about it is the fact that, through the forces of the human soul, what is organic in nature can be metamorphosed into soul nature! If everything we can possess through the activity of our earthly organism is rightly transformed by us after it has become warmth, it then transmutes itself in the soul into what we may call an inner, living experience of compassion, an interest in all other beings. If we penetrate through all the processes of the human organism to the highest level of all, to the processes of warmth, we pass as it were through the door of human physiological processes ... into the world where the warmth of the blood gains worth in relation to what our soul makes of it, to the extent that the soul develops living interest for all existence, and compassion for everything around it. In this way, if our inner life carries us on to a kindling of inner heat, we broaden our life beyond all earthly existence. And we must comprehend the wonderful fact that the whole of cosmic existence has first taken the round-about path of developing our whole organism in order finally to give us that warmth we must transmute through our I into living compassion for all beings.

In the earth's mission, warmth is in the process of being transmuted into compassion.

This is the meaning of Earth evolution; and it is being fulfilled ... through the fact that all physical processes finally come together in our organism as their crown; that everything in it, as a microcosm of all earthly processes, opens again into new blossoming. And as this is transmuted in the human soul, our interest and living compassion for every kind of being enables the earth organism to attain the goal for which warmth was assigned us as beings on earth. What we absorb into our souls through living interest, helping us broaden our inner soul life more and more, will accompany us as we pass through many transformations[50] so that we can use to the full, for the spirit, all that the earth can give us as kindling heat, burning warmth, flame of fire! And when, after all these incarnations we have absorbed into ourselves all possible fervour of warmth, the earth will have reached its goal and purpose. Then it will sink beneath us, a great corpse, into inchoate cosmic space . . . Just as the individual human being, after passing through the gateway of death, advances to new incarnations, so will the throng of all individual souls, after the earth corpse has fallen away, advance to new planetary stages of existence.[51]

And so we find that nothing is lost in the cosmos, but that what is given us within our human organism up to the final blossoming of heat is the 'material' which, when we have used it up as burning warmth, helps us to find the way to a new and higher stage leading to eternity. Nothing in the world is lost, but what the earth produces, through human souls, is carried on by them into eternity!

Notes

1. Johann Wolfgang von Goethe, *Der Versuch als Vermittler von Objekt und Subjekt*, 1793.
2. In Steiner's view we possess, apart from our mineralized physical body, an etheric or life body which we share with the plant kingdom, and an astral or soul body which we have in common with animals. The etheric body is chiefly associated with rhythms, circulation and habitual ways of doing things, while the astral body is the seat of passions, emotions and soul. The fourth, and eternal, aspect of our being is the 'I' or ego which continues to exist after death and subsequently seeks reincarnation in a new body.
3. Note by Steiner: Anyone who objects that a microscopic examination would reveal the difference between the real seed and the imitation only shows he has failed to grasp the point. The aim of the exercise is not to examine the object as seen by the physical senses, but to use it in order to develop forces of soul and spirit.
4. Anthroposophy was the name Steiner gave to his wide-ranging, Christ-centred philosophy and practice. Literally it means 'wisdom of the human being'.
5. One might also, of course, say 'environmental issues'.
6. See note 2 above.
7. The span of human life used to be regarded as 'three score years and ten', or 70.
8. See note 2 above.
9. A higher realm of cosmic intelligence.
10. See note 2 above.
11. See note 2 above.
12. In other words, pliable and flexible.
13. Steiner was speaking to workmen building the first 'Goetheanum' at the headquarters of the Anthroposophical Society in Dornach, Switzerland.

14. See note 2 above.

15. See note 2 above, and introduction to this section.

16. See section 7.

17. See note 2 above.

18. See page 103.

19. See, for instance: Maria Thun, *The Biodynamic Year*, Rudolf Steiner Press, 2007.

20. See, for instance: Lawrence Edwards, *The Vortex of Life*, Floris Books, 1993.

21. Shakespeare's *The Tempest* gives a vivid picture of the enchantment of an elemental being Ariel, though in this case his master Prospero intentionally maintains the enchantment for his own ends. Release for Ariel does eventually come at the end of the play.

22. A recent article in the *Observer* magazine stated: 'But scientists now know the world is not so simple. While a brick weighs as much as the atoms inside it, according to the best theory physicists have ... the basic building blocks inside atoms weigh nothing at all. As matter is broken down to ever smaller constituents, from molecule to atoms to quarks, mass appears to evaporate before our eyes. Physicists have never understood why.' (17.11.07)

23. Imagination, inspiration and intuition are three perceptive faculties which a human being can consciously develop. See: Rudolf Steiner, *Occult Science. An Outline*.

24. See note 2 above.

25. See Ariel's Song in *The Tempest* by William Shakespeare: 'Where the bee sucks, there suck I ...'

26. The forces of gravity are of course centred in the earth, and as such 'gravitate' towards it. What Steiner presumably means here is that the plant creates and is created out of a fusion between earth and cosmic forces. The former rise up in the plant in the sense that it bears physical matter up towards the cosmos.

27. Parasitic only in the sense that Steiner here conceives the leaves and flowers of a tree as being, as it were, grafted on the trunk, and more separate from the earth than is the case in a herbaceous plant.

28. Steiner details these relationships elsewhere in this lecture, in passages not included here.

29. *Aristida stricta* and *Aristida oligantha*. Both varieties are called 'ant grass'.

30. This word had not yet been coined in Steiner's time. The German word he uses is *Haushalt*, which means, roughly, 'balance and interaction'.

31. Steiner was speaking to workmen building the first 'Goetheanum' at the headquarters of the Anthroposophical Society in Dornach, Switzerland.

32. See note 2 above.

33. See extract on page 116.

34. This is not necessarily contradicted by the fact that the beaver uses its tail as a paddle when swimming, to keep its balance on land, and to warn others of approaching danger. The 'accumulated intelligence' Steiner speaks of could also act in these ways.

35. Karma allows us to evolve by presenting us with situations that belong to us (due to our actions or thoughts in past lives) so that we can try to transform them.

36. Sainfoin (*Onobrychis viciifolia*) is a leguminous crop grown for hay and pasturage.

37. See note 2 above.

38. About a third of an acre.

39. See page 178.

40. See page 150.

41. For details, see: Joseph Werr, *Tierzucht und Tiermedizin im Rahmen biologisch-dynamischer Landwirtschaft*, Stuttgart 1953.

42. This, of course, is already starting to happen.

43. Otto Weininger, 1880–1903. Weininger committed suicide at the age of 23.

44. There was unusually thick fog in London at the time.

45. See also: Rudolf Steiner, *The Interior of the Earth*, Rudolf Steiner Press, 2007.

46. The Lemurian epoch was the third epoch of the earth, preceding the fourth or Atlantean epoch. The latter ended with the 'Great Flood' and we are now in the fifth or 'post-Atlantean' era, the midpoint of which was embodied in Greek and Roman culture and the time of Christ.

47. Lucifer and Ahriman are the two polar forces of evil in Steiner's cosmology. Lucifer tempts us away from the earth while Ahriman fetters us to it. Christ is the balancing mediator between these two.

48. See note 31 above.

49. The consciousness soul is a state of objective, onlooker consciousness and mature responsibility, one perhaps typified at present by swiftly developing awareness of the need to care for the planet and counteract the dangers of global warming.

50. Steiner is referring to reincarnation: the repeated rebirth of the individual human spirit in different epochs of evolution.

51. After our current fifth post-Atlantean epoch, which Steiner says will end with the 'war of all against all', two further epochs will follow before the dissolution of the earth and its entry into 'pralaya' prior to a new planetary incarnation. This does not mean, however, that it is of no consequence whether we destroy the conditions for human life on the globe prematurely. To do so would deprive us—and the creatures and beings with which we share the planet—of the means to complete a necessary process of evolution. The editor of this volume has no idea what the consequences of this would be for our future, but presumes it would be disastrous.

Sources

Numbers relate to section numbers in this volume.

1. In: *Theosophy*, Anthroposophic Press, 1994
2. In: *Theosophy*, Anthroposophic Press, 1994
3. In: *Knowledge of the Higher Worlds*, Rudolf Steiner Press, 1969
4. Vienna, 1 October 1923, in: *Michaelmas and the Soul Forces of Man*, Anthroposophic Press, 1982
5. Koberwitz, Silesia, 14 June 1924, in: *Agriculture*, Biodynamic Farming and Gardening Association Inc., 1993
6. (i) Dornach, 12 April 1924, in: *From Beetroot to Buddhism*, Rudolf Steiner Press, 1999
   (ii) St Gallen, 16 November 1917, in: *Secret Brotherhoods*, Rudolf Steiner Press, 2004
   (iii) Berlin, 30 March 1918, in: 'The Earth as a Being with Life, Soul and Spirit' (GA 181), *www.rsarchive.org*
   (iv) Dornach, 9 May 1920, in: *Mystery of the Universe*, Rudolf Steiner Press, 2001
7. (i) Dornach, 31 March 1923, in: *The Cycle of the Year*, Anthroposophic Press, 1984
   (ii) Dornach, 2 May 1920, in: *Mystery of the Universe*, Rudolf Steiner Press, 2001
8. Dornach, 16 April 1920, in: *Mystery of the Universe*, Rudolf Steiner Press, 2001
9. Stuttgart, 6 August 1908, in: *Universe, Earth and Man*, Rudolf Steiner Press, 1987
10. Dornach, 2 February 1924, in: *Anthroposophy and the Inner Life*, Rudolf Steiner Press, 1992
11. Dornach, 17 April 1920, in: *Mystery of the Universe*, Rudolf Steiner Press, 2001
12. Dornach, 9 February 1924, in: *From Elephants to Einstein*, Rudolf Steiner Press, 1998

13. Dornach, 28 October 1923, in: *Harmony of the Creative Word*, Rudolf Steiner Press, 2001

14. (i) Berlin, 8 December 1920, in: *The Spirit in the Realm of Plants*, Anthroposophic Press, 1984
    (ii) Dornach, 9 August 1924, in: *From Sunspots to Strawberries*, Rudolf Steiner Press, 2002

15. (i) Dornach, 23 September 1922, in: *From Crystals to Crocodiles*, Rudolf Steiner Press, 2002
    (ii) Dornach, 31 July 1924, in: *From Sunspots to Strawberries*, Rudolf Steiner Press, 2002

16. Dornach, 10 November 1923, in: *Harmony of the Creative Word*, Rudolf Steiner Press, 2001

17. (i) Vienna, 28 September 1923, in: *Michaelmas and the Soul Forces of Man*, Anthroposophic Press, 1982
    (ii) Dornach, 2 November 1923, in: *Harmony of the Creative Word*, Rudolf Steiner Press, 2001

18. Koberwitz, Silesia, 15 June 1924, in: *Agriculture*, Biodynamic Farming and Gardening Association Inc., 1993

19. (i) Dornach, 26 October 1923, in: *Harmony of the Creative Word*, Rudolf Steiner Press, 2001
    (ii) Dornach, 19 October 1923, in: *Harmony of the Creative Word*, Rudolf Steiner Press, 2001

20. Dornach, 5 January 1923, in: *From Comets to Cocaine*, Rudolf Steiner Press, 2000

21. Dornach, 15 December 1923, in: *Bees*, Anthroposophic Press, 1998

22. (i) Dornach, 26 November 1923, in: *Bees*, Anthroposophic Press, 1998
    (ii) Dornach, 10 December 1923, in: *Bees*, Anthroposophic Press, 1998
    (iii) Dornach, 1 December 1923, in: *Bees*, Anthroposophic Press, 1998
    (iv) Dornach, 5 December 1923, in: *Bees*, Anthroposophic Press, 1998

(v) Dornach, 3 February 1923, in: *From Comets to Cocaine*, Rudolf Steiner Press, 2000

23. Dornach, 19 October 1923, in: *Harmony of the Creative Word*, Rudolf Steiner Press, 2001

24. Koberwitz, Silesia, 12 June 1924, in: *Agriculture*, Biodynamic Farming and Gardening Association Inc., 1993

25. Dornach, 10 January 1923, in: *From Comets to Cocaine*, Rudolf Steiner Press, 2000

26. (i) Hamburg, 17 May 1910, in: *Manifestations of Karma*, Rudolf Steiner Press, 2000
(ii) Cologne, 7 June 1908, in: *The Festivals and their Meaning*, Rudolf Steiner Press, 2002

27. Torquay, 14 August 1924, in: *The Kingdom of Childhood*, Rudolf Steiner Press, 1995

28. (i) Koberwitz, Silesia, 10 June 1924, in: *Agriculture*, Biodynamic Farming and Gardening Association Inc., 1993
(ii) Koberwitz, Silesia, 13 June 1924, in: *Agriculture Course*, Rudolf Steiner Press, 2004

29. Koberwitz, Silesia, 11 June 1924, in: *Agriculture*, Biodynamic Farming and Gardening Association Inc., 1993

30. (i) Dornach, 5 December 1923, in: *Bees*, Anthroposophic Press, 1998
(ii) Dornach, 13 January 1923, in: *From Comets to Cocaine*, Rudolf Steiner Press, 2000
(iii) Koberwitz, Silesia, 16 June 1924, in: *Agriculture*, Biodynamic Farming and Gardening Association Inc., 1993
(iv) Dornach, 9 October 1920 (notes from conversation), in: *Agriculture*, Biodynamic Farming and Gardening Association Inc., 1993

31. (i) Dornach, 20 October 1923, in: *Harmony of the Creative Word*, Rudolf Steiner Press, 2001
(ii) Dornach, 25 November 1917, in: *Secret Brotherhoods*, Rudolf Steiner Press, 2004
(iii) Koberwitz, Silesia, 16 June 1924, in: *Agriculture*, Bio-

dynamic Farming and Gardening Association Inc., 1993

(iv) Stuttgart, 11 June 1923, in: GA 345 (not translated)

32. (i) Dornach, 30 July 1916, in: *Riddle of Humanity*, Rudolf Steiner Press, 1990

(ii) London, 16 November 1922, in: *Planetary Spheres and their Influence*, Rudolf Steiner Press, 1982

(iii) Paris, 12 June 1906, in: *An Esoteric Cosmology*, St George Publications, 1978

(iv) Berlin, 1 January 1909, in: *The Deed of Christ and the Opposing Spiritual Powers*, Steiner Book Centre, 1976

33. (i) Stuttgart, 13 October 1922, in: *Becoming the Archangel Michael's Companions*, SteinerBooks, 2007

(ii) Oslo, Whitsun 1923, in: *Man's Being, His Destiny and World Evolution*, Anthroposophic Press, 1983

34. Prague, 28 March 1911, in: *Occult Physiology*, Rudolf Steiner Press, 1983

Further Reading

Rudolf Steiner's fundamental books:

Knowledge of the Higher Worlds
also published as: *How to Know Higher Worlds*

Occult Science
also published as: *An Outline of Esoteric Science*

Theosophy

The Philosophy of Freedom
also published as:
Intuitive Thinking as a Spiritual Path

Some relevant volumes of Rudolf Steiner's lectures:

Agriculture Course
Bees
Harmony of the Creative Word
Mystery of the Universe
Universe, Earth and Man

For all titles contact Rudolf Steiner Press (UK) or
SteinerBooks (USA):
www.rudolfsteinerpress.com www.steinerbooks.org

Note on Rudolf Steiner's Lectures

The lectures and addresses contained in this volume have been translated from the German, which is based on stenographic and other recorded texts that were in most cases never seen or revised by the lecturer. Hence, due to human errors in hearing and transcription, they may contain mistakes and faulty passages. Every effort has been made to ensure that this is not the case. Some of the lectures were given to audiences more familiar with anthroposophy; these are the so-called 'private' or 'members' lectures. Other lectures, like the written works, were intended for the general public. The difference between these, as Rudolf Steiner indicates in his *Autobiography*, is twofold. On the one hand, the members' lectures take for granted a background in and commitment to anthroposophy; in the public lectures this was not the case. At the same time, the members' lectures address the concerns and dilemmas of the members, while the public work arises from, and directly addresses Steiner's own understanding of universal needs. Nevertheless, as Rudolf Steiner stresses: 'Nothing was ever said that was not solely the result of my direct experience of the growing content of anthroposophy. There was never any question of concessions to the prejudices and preferences of the members. Whoever reads these privately printed lectures can take them to represent anthroposophy in the fullest sense. Thus it was possible without hesitation—when the complaints in this direction became too persistent—to depart from the custom of circulating this material "For members only". But it must be borne in mind that faulty passages do occur in these reports not revised by myself.' Earlier in the same chapter, he states: 'Had I been able to correct them [*the private lectures*], the restriction *for members only* would have been unnecessary from the beginning.' The original German editions on which this text is based were published by Rudolf Steiner Verlag, Dornach, Switzerland in the collected edition

(*Gesamtausgabe*, 'GA') of Rudolf Steiner's work. All publications are edited by the Rudolf Steiner Nachlassverwaltung (estate), which wholly owns both Rudolf Steiner Verlag and the Rudolf Steiner Archive.

Rudolf Steiner
Nature Spirits
Selected Lectures

Based on knowledge attained through his highly-trained clairvoyance, Rudolf Steiner contends that folk traditions regarding nature spirits are based on spiritual reality. He describes how people possessed a natural spiritual vision in ancient times, enabling them to commune with nature spirits. These entities—which are also referred to as elemental beings—became immortalised as fairies and gnomes in myth, legend and children's stories.

Today, says Steiner, the instinctive understanding that humanity once had for these elemental beings should be transformed into clear scientific knowledge. He even asserts that humanity will not be able to reconnect with the spiritual world if it cannot develop a new relationship to the elementals. The nature spirits themselves want to be of great assistance to us, acting as 'emissaries of higher divine spiritual beings'.

ISBN 978 1 85584 018 8; 208pp; £12.95

Rudolf Steiner
Evil
Selected Lectures

Despite the fact that evil is an omnipresent theme of our age, it remains one of the most problematic. Public references to it are continually made, but to what extent has society truly begun to understand its riddle?

In this selection of insightful lectures Rudolf Steiner addresses the subject of evil from the results of his spiritual research, offering an original and complex picture. He describes evil as a phenomenon which arises when a thing appears outside its true context, enabling something which is initially 'good' to become harmful. He speaks of the effect of particular spiritual beings—principally Lucifer and Ahriman—who work as polar forces, laying hindrances in our path. Yet, paradoxically, confronting and coming to terms with such difficulties ultimately furthers our development. Thus Steiner speaks of evil as a necessary phenomenon in human evolution, allowing for the possibility of freedom.

ISBN 978 1 85584 046 1; 224pp; £11.95

Rudolf Steiner
Self-Transformation
Selected Lectures

At the heart of Rudolf Steiner's spiritual philosophy is the path of inner development leading to personal transformation. Steiner shows how, through specific meditative exercises, it is possible to break out of the restricted world of everyday consciousness. He gives advice on the development of inner qualities such as clear thinking, inner tranquillity and positivity, which lay a necessary foundation for esoteric work.

In contrast to many of the New Age paths available today, Steiner's methods are based on the Western tradition, the Rosicrucian path of initiation, as opposed to older Eastern teachings. This modern way, he suggests, is a metamorphosis of the Eastern paths and is best suited to modern consciousness. Speaking as an initiate, he describes the levels of attainment on this spiritual journey, the first being 'imagination' where the spiritual world is revealed in pictures, followed by 'inspiration' and finally 'intuition'.

ISBN 978 1 85584 019 5; 256pp; £12.95

Rudolf Steiner
Angels
Selected Lectures

Religious and spiritual writings have always made reference
to beings from the spiritual hierarchies, especially those
known in Christian tradition as Angels. These spirits are the
closest to human beings and act as our invisible guides and
companions. They influence the life of the individual as well
as the evolution of humanity and the cosmos.

From his own clairvoyant vision Rudolf Steiner confirmed
the existence of such spiritual beings, and showed how
modern minds could gain access to their world. As he
explains in these inspiring lectures, it is important for us to
understand and cooperate with the work of the Angels today
as this is crucial for the further development of humanity.

ISBN 978 1 85584 060 7; 192pp; £11.95